*To Marcelo with every warm
wish always, in all ways*

[signature]

A TREASURY
OF
SHABBAT INSPIRATION

A TREASURY
OF
SHABBAT INSPIRATION

Rabbi Sidney Greenberg

with a foreword by
Rabbi Harold M. Schulweis

**THE UNITED SYNAGOGUE OF
CONSERVATIVE JUDAISM**
Commission on Jewish Education

ACKNOWLEDGEMENTS
Acknowledgements and copyrights may be found on page 132, which constitutes an extension of the copyright page.

ISBN # 0-8381-3119-0

Cover Illustration. Challah cover. Embroidered cotton. American or European, 19th-20th c. Jewish Museum/Art Resource, New York, U.S.A.

Dedication

This book is dedicated to two of my very dear friends, the late

Milton Newman

who was always there for anyone in need, and

Ida Newman

a woman of strength and dignity who acts with kindness and courage, and with gratitude to their loving nephews and nieces.

TABLE OF CONTENTS

Foreword

Rabbi Sidney Greenberg's loving anthology embraces the wholeness of the Sabbath, the Jewish passion for unity. In it the two wines and two lights of *Kiddush* and *Havdalah* flow into each other.

"The owl of Minerva flies only at dusk." Hegel, in this poetic insight, maintained that wisdom is retrospective. We learn by looking back. At *havdalah* we look back to the Sabbath to understand its fuller meaning. We wait for the three stars at the conclusion of the *Shabbat* to illumine the Sabbath that has passed. In the play of *Havdalah* light over the fingers of our opened hand, the kindling of the Friday evening Sabbath lights takes on deeper meaning.

The Sabbath begins with candles and wine and ends with wine and candles. *Kiddush* and *Havdalah* belong together, a complementary reflection of the complexity and unity of creation.

Taken whole, the Sabbath is the diastole and systole of the heart. After releasing the contractions of acquisition and relaxing the muscles that squeeze the earth throughout the week, we are enabled to return reinvigorated to the task of transforming the environment. "Six days shalt thou labor and do all thy work" is essential to the mandate to keep the seventh day as "a Sabbath unto the Lord thy God." Seven days of labor or seven days of rest would rupture the wholeness of the body-soul. One cannot live by work alone nor can one live by rest alone.

Everything is connected. Nothing is to be sundered forever. The *Havdalah* prayer celebrates the nexus: the sacred and the profane, light and darkness, Israel and the nations of the world, the seventh day and the sixth day of labor are polarities that belong to each other.

Kiddush and *Havdalah*, two different cups of wine, two separate candles of light, are interdependent. Both are reminders of creation, both know the secret of creation — separation, differentiation, discernment. Throughout the opening chapter of Genesis, God's acts of creation are repeatedly punctuated as acts of division. The reiterated verb is *"va'yavdayl"* (and God divided) —dividing light from darkness, the waters under the firmament from the waters above the firmament, land from ocean, sun from moon, cattle from creeping things, beast from fowl and fishes. *Kiddush* means consecration, *Havdalah* means separation. To consecrate is to set apart.

Creativity entails discernment. The prayer in praise of wisdom is prologue and epilogue in the silent prayer at the conclusion of the Sabbath. "You endow human beings with knowledge and teach them discernment — *"binah."* *"Binah,"* the Hebrew term for discernment, is related to the Hebrew term *"bayn"* which means between. On the Sabbath we experience the joy and wisdom of betweenness, the relationship between each other, between the environment and ourselves, between the external self and the internal self, between the body and soul. On the Sabbath we hold together that which we have differentiated, not allowing creation to be fragmented but recognizing the marvel of its interdependence.

Light and shadow, fear and love are interrelated. The lights of *Havdalah* themselves were created out of death and despair. In the Midrash (Genesis Rabbah 11:2) we are told that the light which God created the first day lit up the world from the time Adam was created until the sunset of the following day. That night after the Sabbath, the sun disappeared and with it its warmth and light. The shadows lengthened over the freshly formed earth and the first man was filled with dread. He feared that his creation would be short lived, that he was experiencing the death of the world. As he threw himself upon the ground, his hands fell upon two stones. Upon one stone was written the term *"afelah,"* darkness, on the other stone was written the Hebrew word *"mavet,"* death. He rubbed both stones together until fire was produced and lit a torch that protected him from the darkness of the night. At dawn, Adam saw the sun appear and concluded "This is the way of the world. The sun sinks but it will rise again." The twisted candle of multiple lights is raised to celebrate the transcendent triumph over fear and darkness. The hand that was closed on the Sabbath, prohibited from handling fire, is opened to help shape God's incompleted world in the weekly cycle of labor and repair.

Arm in arm, awaiting Elijah, we sing a song of the *Havdalah*.

Black into white
light into shadow
Blessing into curse
Doubt into belief.

Nothing comes divided
neatly severed
cut off
one half from another
Trimmed polarities.

Nothing is given pure, simple, unalloyed.
Nothing is given in halves
Except - idolatries.
In strange worship
halves and quarters
pretend wholeness.
A small coin held close to the eye
blocks out the world
and everything appears draped in darkness.

Simple solutions
blur distinctions
confusing blindness
with wholeness.

Light and shadow
sweet and bitter
the admixture is inseparable.

Accept it whole
fragrance and galbanum
together
elements of sanctified incense.

Accept it whole
yet not without distinction.
Ours is not theirs
day is not night.

Accept it whole
but not with cruel division
that amputates organic wholeness.

Accept it whole
without the conceit of absorption
that swallows
the shadow side with light.

Accept it whole
not renting cloth
into convenient rags
sundering the universe
into segregated parts:
Good or evil
Week or Sabbath
Them or us.

Divisions desecrate
Hard disjunctives
rip apart
the underlying unity,
the possibility of reconciliation.

Hallow the link between
darkness and light
mundane and festive
others and us.
Hallow the circles
that demark separate styles.
Hallow the outer lines
that penetrate each other
without assimilation.

Creation and separation
Kiddush and *Havdalah*
different wines
different candles.
Shabbat Shalom
Shavua Tov.

Harold M. Shulweis
5755/1994

Introduction

Three great loves motivated me to create this *Shabbat* Anthology.

The first of these is my love for the *Shabbat* itself. If I might paraphrase the words of the poet, I would say, "Why do I love thee, let me count the ways." *Shabbat* is indeed one of God's most precious gifts to us, so special that it was the only ritual injunction included in the Ten Commandments.

Shabbat appears in different versions in the two places in the Torah where the Commandments are proclaimed. In the Book of Exodus, *Shabbat* is a reminder of God's creation of the world. In the Book of Deuteronomy, the *Shabbat* is linked to God's liberation of our ancestors from Egyptian slavery. These two themes, creation and liberation, are woven into the very fabric of this holy day.

By reminding ourselves every seventh day of God's creative power, a power which God shared with us, we are motivated to become partners with God in the on-going work of creation. Ours is the divine task of making our individual contribution "to perfect the world into a Kingdom of God" — to use the liturgical phrase of the *Aleinu* with which we conclude each of the three daily services. God has given us the power to create with our hands, our hearts and our minds. It is this power that we are to use during the six days of the week.

In the Book of Deuteronomy we are urged to keep *Shabbat* in order to "remember that you were a slave in the land of Egypt and the Lord your God brought you forth from there." Thus, *Shabbat* became a messenger of liberation urging us to free ourselves from care and anxiety; from anger and strife. To utter words of rebuke on *Shabbat* is the emotional equivalent of the act of lighting a fire — explicitly prohibited by the Torah.

James Truslow Adams, the American historian, wrote: "Perhaps it would be a good idea, fantastic as it sounds, to muffle every telephone, halt every motor, and stop all activity some day, to give people a chance to ponder for a few minutes on what it is all about, why they are living and what they really want."

Adams might have been surprised to learn that this "good idea" is not at all "fantastic." Long ago this idea was incorporated in a day which comes every week. We call it "*Shabbat*."

On this day we greet one another with the words *Shabbat* Shalom — "may *Shabbat* bring you peace." Peace and serenity are among the gifts this day brings into our lives, together with joy and delight. It is a day for inner quiet, a day to rediscover our human dignity. *Shabbat* helps us to liberate ourselves from the tyranny of the clock and the calendar. It provides us with a weekly exodus from the world of strain, struggle and strife.

If we want to grasp the benevolent influence of the Sabbath we have to see how it impacts on the lives of people who observe it. A number of illustrations rush to mind. Henrietta Szold, the founder of Hadassah, would begin her day at 4:30 AM, end it at midnight, and work busily all the intervening hours. When a close friend once asked her how she was able to work this way, she answered: "There are two reasons: one, I keep the Sabbath; and two, my cast iron stomach." She went on to add that when she lit her candles on Friday, she put aside all business and cares and entered into the pure delight of the *Shabbat*. This day renewed her for the week ahead.

Sam Levenson, the celebrated comedian, once gave us a remarkable insight into what *Shabbat* meant to the ordinary Jew, the Jew who struggled to eke out a living. Writing of his father, he tells us: "Now when it came to Papa, he dealt in two times: sacred time and profane time. Making a living, being a sweatshop slave 16 hours a day, this was profane time. But came '*Erev Shabbos*' with the candles lit on the table, and I could see my father change from a sweatshop slave into an angelic figure who had something to do with eternity and sacred time. Suddenly the wrinkles came out of his face, and he became again a holy man who was related to the whole universe and to God's destiny for man — which was greater than sitting over a sewing machine in a sweatshop."

What *Shabbat* has done for Henrietta Szold and Sam Levenson's father it can do for every Jew. In these harried, hurried and harassed times we urgently require some of the spiritual and emotional healing *Shabbat* benevolently offers.

Moreover, our *Shabbat* can make a powerful contribution to preserving the integrity of the Jewish family. At a time when so many challenges confront the cohesiveness of the Jewish family, we can ill afford to dispense with the binding impact *Shabbat* provides.

The second love that motivated the creation of this anthology was my love for my people and our heritage. I am persuaded that one of the strongest factors enabling the Jew to survive creatively in the past has been the observance of *Shabbat*. I am equally persuaded that, if Judaism is to survive in the future, it will be the *Shabbat* that will provide the same staying power.

Cyrus Adler captured this truth in words worth remembering: "If I were asked to single out one of the great historical institutions more essential for our preservation than all others, I would not hesitate to declare that it is the observance of the Sabbath. Without this, the home and the synagogue, the festivals and the holy days, the language and the history of our people would gradually disappear. If the Sabbath will be maintained by those who have observed it, and will be restored to those who have abandoned it, then the permanence of Judaism is assured."

The third love which moved me to bring together in one volume all the blessings *Shabbat* brings, was my love of God. The *Shabbat* itself is regarded as a sign of God's love for us. This theme recurs in our Sabbath liturgy.

Just as a beloved looks upon an engagement ring and thinks of the lover who presented it to her, so do we think of the Giver of *Shabbat* when we immerse ourselves in its spirit and enjoy its richness.

The *Shabbat* is called "a sign forever between Me and the children of Israel." It is the enduring link between us and our God.

On *Shabbat* we are granted an "added soul," a *neshamah yiteirah,* and it is this expanded soul which rejoices in its God. The *Shabbat* candles which we light, the *kiddush* which we recite, the blessings over the food we enjoy, the table songs we sing, the expanded prayers we offer — all celebrate the God of creation and liberation. On no other day of the week is it as natural to feel the presence of God and gratitude for God's gifts.

It is my fervent prayer that this book will help the readers to develop and to deepen within themselves the three loves which brought it into existence.

Editor's Note

I am grateful to my good friend Rabbi Jonathan D. Levine of Media Judaica, the co-editor of my liturgical works. His editorial skill is especially evident in the prayers which appear over my name — originally published in the volumes on which we collaborated.

Sidney Greenberg

1

A Precious Gift
From God

Wolpert, Ludwig. Kiddush Cup. Jerusalem, 1964. Silver, hammered and
engraved, 19.1 cm. high. Museum purchase, JM 67-64. Jewish Museum/
Art Resource, New York, U. S.A.

HOW A SWEATSHOP SLAVE
BECAME A HOLY PERSON

Sam Levenson, the celebrated comedian, once gave us a remarkable insight into what *Shabbat* meant to the ordinary Jew, the Jew who struggled to eke out a living. Writing of his father, he tells us:

"Now when it came to Papa, he dealt in two times: sacred time and profane time. Making a living, being a sweatshop slave 16 hours a day, this was profane time. But came '*Erev Shabbos*' with the candles lit on the table, I could see my father change from a sweatshop slave into an angelic figure who had something to do with eternity and sacred time.

"Suddenly the wrinkles came out of his face, and he became again a holy man who was related to the whole universe and to God's destiny for man — which was greater than sitting over a sewing machine."

Sidney Greenberg
Lessons for Living

AN ISLAND OF STILLNESS

The world has our hands, but our soul belongs to Someone Else. Six days a week we seek to dominate the world, on the seventh day we try to dominate the self....

To set apart one day a week for freedom, a day on which we would not use the instruments which have been so easily turned into weapons of destruction, a day for being with ourselves, a day of detachment from the vulgar, of independence of external obligations, a day on which we stop worshipping the idols of technical civilization, a day on which we use no money, a day of armistice in the economic struggle with our fellow men and the forces of nature — is there any institution that holds out a greater hope for man's progress than the Sabbath?

In the tempestuous ocean of time and toil there are islands of stillness where man may enter a harbor and reclaim our dignity. The island is the seventh day, the Sabbath, a day of detachment from things, instruments and practical affairs as well as of attachment to the spirit.

Abraham J. Heschel
The Sabbath

GOD'S MOST PRECIOUS GIFT TO ISRAEL

One story in the Talmud tells that when Moses went up to Mount Sinai, God said to him:

"I have a precious gift in My treasury, and I wish to present it to Israel."

"Is it the Ten Commandments?" asked Moses.

"I shall give them the Commandments too," said God. "But this is a different gift."

"Is it the Sacred Books of the Law?" asked Moses.

"I shall give them the Sacred Books of the Law also," said God. "But this is a different gift."

"Is it the Holy of Holies in the Temple of Jerusalem?" asked Moses.

"I shall give them the Holy of Holies in the Temple of Jerusalem," said God. "But this gift is even more precious."

"What can it be?" asked Moses.

"It is the Sabbath," said God.

Joseph Gaer & Alfred Wolf
Our Jewish Heritage

LIFE IS WORTHWHILE

Shabbat represents the affirmation that life is not vain or futile, but supremely worthwhile.

Mordecai M. Kaplan
(adapted)

A SURE FIRE PRESCRIPTION

We must be re-educated to realize the value of the *Shabbat*. It's not the Sabbath which is behind the time. It is we in America who are still behind in this achievement.

Hayim Donin
Beyond Thyself

SHABBAT UNIFIES THE RITUAL AND THE ETHICAL

According to classical Judaism, ethics is the way to serve God; ritual is the way to connect to God. *Shabbat* unifies the two aspects in one experience.

Irving Greenberg
The Jewish Way — Living the Holidays

SHABBAT NURTURES OUR NOBILITY

The proper observance of *Shabbat*, the Rabbis said, enables one to experience a "sixtieth" of what is in store for the righteous in the future world or in the Messianic era. It is to catch a glimpse of what the world was like, before Adam sinned, and what it can be again if we learn to observe God's law. Such observance of *Shabbat* nurtures and exercises our noblest intellectual and emotional endowments, and constitutes the closest approximation thus far achieved to the concretization in act of the concepts of the Kingdom of God, of the equality before God of all of His creatures, of the human being as a creature made in God's image, and of the achievability of the purpose for which God in love created the universe.

Simon Greenberg
A Jewish Philosophy and Pattern of Life

A DAY FOR THE BODY AND THE SOUL

The Sabbath reconciles, showing us how to enlist the desires of the body and turn them to noble ends, how to capture the "evil urge" and bring it under the realm of the holy, how to sanctify the common. For the Sabbath is not a day for the soul alone, it was meant for the body as well. "And Moses said, 'Eat it today, for a Sabbath is this day unto the Lord'" (Exodus 16:25). Rabbi Zerika, a Talmudic sage, explains this verse to mean that from this we learn "that one should have three meals on the Sabbath" (*Shabbat* 117b). Holiness does not mean removal from the world but sanctification of the worldly. We are not required to become ascetics on the Seventh Day; our physical demands are not denied. What happens, however, is that on the Sabbath, these physical demands become *mitzvot* and are transformed into something in which God too has a share, in which there is divine concern. Food, wine, marital relations, all of them fleshly desires, become *mitzvot* on the Sabbath. Thus the passions are sanctified, the "evil urge" is transformed and enlisted in the divine cause.

Samuel H. Dresner
The Sabbath

PREPARING FOR A SPECIAL GUEST

The holy *Shabbat* is the greatest gift given us by the Holy One. So we should rejoice in the coming of *Shabbat*. If the expectation of a special guest would cause us to prepare with great care, how much more so should we act when the guest is the *Shabbat* Bride. Fresh coverings should be set aside for Friday evening. Something special should even be eaten on *Shabbat*. Everyone, even someone with servants, must do something himself to honor *Shabbat* whether it be helping prepare the meal, cleaning the house, or purchasing flowers to adorn the *Shabbat* table.

Joseph Caro
Shulhan Aruh

TAKING TIME OUT

To me *Shabbat* is full of beautiful memories. But even more than that, it's when I try to make time in my life to think and to meditate. I really feel that the concept of taking time out of your life to think is very fundamental. When I go to *Shul* I'm not always exactly following the service. I sit and say, I need some place which is dedicated to eternity. That is why I go to the synagogue. How many places will I find like this? I won't find it in a nightclub. I won't find it on the streets. Other than *Shul*, there's no other place where we still talk about the beginning of things and the end of things.

Sam Levenson
Everything But Money

REST AND GROW

To that part of us which is secular and animal, *Shabbat* says, "rest"; to that part of us which is spiritual, moral, and human, *Shabbat* says, "grow."

Sidney Greenberg

SHABBAT - A GIFT FROM GOD

Despite the truth of most Jewish and non-Jewish defenses of rest and recreation, the *Shabbat* without God, without recognition that it is a Divine gift and not merely a human therapy, is grossly and pitifully fragmented.

Elliot B. Gertel

WHY IS THE SABBATH CALLED A BRIDE?

What is the difference between the Christian Sunday and the Jewish Sabbath? One way to distinguish them is to ask yourself whether Sunday, now or in the past, could be transformed into a person, a bride. Sunday is followed by Monday, Tuesday, and so forth, each day having a special name and standing by itself. But to Jews only the seventh day — the Sabbath — has a name, the others but a number. Thus: the "first day," the "second day," or the "third day," in accordance with how near or far they are to the "seventh day." Sunday is a day of commencement, the beginning of a week of toil. The Sabbath is a day of completion, the end of a week of yearning. Sunday arrives at midnight when the world sleeps; it is received passively, automatically. But Jews must "make" Sabbath; they must prepare for it, for the bride will not show her face unless she is invited and loved.

Samuel H. Dresner
The Sabbath

SHABBAT— A SAMPLE

When God was about to give the Torah to Israel He summoned the people and said to them: "My children, I have something precious that I would like to give you for all time, if you will accept My Torah and observe My Commandments."

The people then asked: "Master of the universe, what is that precious gift You have for us?"

The Holy One, blessed be He, replied, "It is the world to come!"

The people of Israel answered: "Show us a sample of the world to come."

The Holy One, blessed be He, said: "The *Shabbat* is a sample of the world to come, for that world will be one long *Shabbat*."

Otiyot d'Rabbi Akiva
letter *Alef*, Quoted in *Likrat Shabbat*

WELCOME TO THE BRIDE

The sixteenth century mystics of Safed created the *Kabbalat Shabbat* Friday evening service. Among the prayers is a beautiful song, "*L'khah Dodi*," an excerpt of which is:

Come my beloved to meet the Bride.
Let us welcome the presence of the Sabbath
Come in peace... and come in joy...
Come, O Bride! Come, O Bride!

To the mystics of Safed, the synagogue was not grand enough to receive the Sabbath: its walls were too limiting, its presence too confining. So they would go out into the open fields, dressed in white, the color of the wedding garment, and there chant psalms and sing *L'khah Dodi,* accompanying the *Shabbat* Bride to their synagogue. Still today, when the last verse of the prayer is sung... the congregation turns from the Ark, faces the entrance and bows to the Bride who is about to enter.

Samuel H. Dresner
The Sabbath

SHABBAT'S MATE

Shabbat complained at Creation that everyone had been created with a mate, except *Shabbat.* God said: "I will give you Israel as your mate."

Genesis Rabbah 11:8

BEYOND CREATION AND REVELATION

The great Sabbath prayer of benediction involves none of those requests that are concerned with the needs of the individual. There are not merely none of the weekday requests for creature comforts, such as a good year, a good harvest, health, intelligence, and good management, but also none of the requests of every child of God for forgiveness of sins, the ultimate redemption. Besides the requests for peace and the coming of the Kingdom — individual as well as community requests — there is only praise and thanks. For on the Sabbath the congregation feels as if it were already redeemed — to the degree such a feeling is at all possible in anticipation. The Sabbath is the feast of creation, but of a creation wrought for the sake of redemption. This feast instituted at the close of creation is creation's meaning and goal. That is why we do not celebrate the festival of the primordial work of creation on the first day of creation, but on its last, on the seventh day.

Franz Rosenzweig
quoted in *Franz Rosenzweig — His Life and Thought*
by Nahum Glatzer

THE FIRST STEP TO THE ABROGATION OF SLAVERY

Had Judaism brought into the world only the Sabbath, it would thereby have proved itself to be a producer of joy and a promoter of peace for mankind. The Sabbath was the first step on the road which led to the abrogation of slavery.

Hermann Cohen
Die Religion der Vernunft

THE SABBATH — OUR GOAL

When a man labors not for a livelihood but to accumulate wealth, then he is a slave. Therefore it is that God granted us the Sabbath. For it is by the Sabbath that we know we are not work animals, born to eat and to labor; we are men. It is the Sabbath which is man's goal — not labor, but the rest which he earns from his labor. It is because the Jews made the Sabbath holy to God that they were redeemed from slavery in Egypt. It was by the Sabbath that they proclaimed that they were not slaves but free men.

Sholem Asch
East River

WHAT *SHABBAT* DOES FOR US

"Those who delight in *Shabbat*" add to their lives
A heritage of "Joy and spiritual distinction."
Shabbat helps us to liberate ourselves
From the tyranny of the clock,
From enslavement to things.
Shabbat provides us with a weekly exodus
From the world of strain, struggle, and strife.
Shabbat summons us to worship and reflect,
To renew our dreams, to rekindle our hopes.
Shabbat drapes us with dignity and honor,
For we are each created in the Divine image.
Shabbat helps us to remember
That we are partners with God in the work of creation.
Shabbat strengthens us for the challenge
To overcome weariness, to resist despair.
Shabbat beckons us to a sense of the holy,
To an awareness of the sacred dimensions of life.
And so we offer our gratitude to God,
Who gave us the *Shabbat*, the most precious of days.

Sidney Greenberg
Siddur Hadash

A WEEKLY GIFT

A Jew by choice was asked whether she misses Christmas. She answered "Christmas is beautiful but it comes once a year. You know how beautiful *Shabbat* is. It comes every single week.

Sidney Greenberg

SHABBAT REMINDS US WE NEED NEVER STAND ALONE

Shabbat is more than a private time for introspection. *Shabbat* is more than a pleasant day away from the office.

Shabbat is an intrinsically Jewish experience, which means that the rest and refreshment of *Shabbat* take on added dimension because they are structured in a Jewish fashion. *Shabbat* allows us to deal with the turmoil of contemporary life in the context of Judaism.

In our society, where the pace of life is hectic and where the moral ground shifts so rapidly, *Shabbat* is important because it can anchor us weekly in ceremonies and values sanctified by centuries of Jewish life.

Shabbat reminds us that Jews need never stand alone. We can always draw our roots in the Jewish experience, our connections to other Jews, our relationship to Torah and the covenant with God.

Mark Dov Shapiro
Gates of Sabbath

WE CAN CONSECRATE OUR TALENTS

It seems odd
to use wine to sanctify the Sabbath.
Wine can intoxicate, confuse the mind.

But *Kiddush* is for lucidity
for twin remembrances
of creation and redemption
of nature that begins with God's word
and of history, the exodus from Egypt

that combines faith and will.
The choice of wine seems odd.
Some deified it, grew drunk on it, cut their flesh
with knives in frenzied piety before pagan gods.
Others spilled wine upon the ground,
prohibiting its use, the squeezed vine of Satan.
But we raise the cup of wine
dedicate it, sanctify the Sabbath through it.

We drink philosophy, a mighty analogue.
As wine is neutral, ambivalent, ambiguous,
as wine is potential, holding in it
the capacity to lose awareness, to desecrate
and the talent to consecrate life,
so all energies that flow from the Creator-Liberator,
can raise up or pull down, rejoice or depress.

Power — this hammer than can knock nails into boards
that holds together homes and hospitals
can ruin the walls of our sanctuaries.
Intelligence — this brain that can discover
and invent cures and continents
can plot and design for death and destruction.

Wealth — this power that can support the fallen
can reduce men and women to slaves,
build shelters for the homeless
or smart bombs to shatter lives.
This wine can rejoice the heart with grand purpose
or render us powerless,
a seductive escape from responsibility.

We raise the wine recalling the seventh day
of creation and the first day of liberation.
We raise the wine to remember the potentiality,
the possibility in us to consecrate our talents
and sanctify our worlds.

Harold M. Schulweis
In God's Mirror

THE *SHABBAT* HAS KEPT US ALIVE

A Jew who feels a real tie with the life of his people throughout the generations will find it utterly impossible to think of the existence of the Jew without the *Shabbat*. One can say without exaggeration that more than the Jew has kept the *Shabbat*, the *Shabbat* has kept the Jew.

Ahad Ha'am

WHEN *SHABBAT* LAWS ARE SET ASIDE

The laws of the *Shabbat* are set aside in cases where there is danger to life, as is the case with all the *mitzvot*. Therefore, a sick person who is in danger may have all his needs taken care of on the *Shabbat* (even when so doing violates the laws of *Shabbat*) if it is so ordered by a doctor. If there is some question as to the seriousness of the illness (as in the case where one doctor says there is danger and another says there is not), then the *Shabbat* is set aside on the principle that, when there is any doubt about danger to life, we set aside the *Shabbat* in order to save life.

Moses Maimonides
Mishneh Torah, Hilkhot Shabbat 11:5

SOME BUSINESS PERMITTED ON THE *SHABBAT*

It is permissible to make plans for good deeds on the Sabbath — one may arrange alms to the poor on Sabbath.... One may transact business which has to do with the saving of life or with public health on Sabbath, and one may go to synagogue to discuss public affairs on Sabbath....

Babylonian Talmud, Shabbat 150A

SHABBAT — GOOD FOR THE HEART

A recent scientific study in Israel demonstrated that non-religious people have a heart-attack risk two and one half times higher than that of religious people.

Can the difference be *Shabbat* observance?

Sidney Greenberg

ENJOYING THE RICHNESS OF JEWISH LIVING

The problem, however, is that the richness of Jewish living is apparent only when you are living it. In this respect, it is no different than most experiences. You can read all you want about parenting, for example, but any parent will tell you that the experience of holding your baby for the first time is something you can't fathom in advance.

The philosopher Franz Rosenzweig described the challenge of conveying Judaism to assimilated Jews as the process of moving from the Jewish periphery to its center. He suggested that people who stand on the outside watching other Jews practice are like deaf people who watch people dance without being able to hear the music to which they are dancing.

A description of the meaning of Yom Kippur, no matter how well it is written, cannot convey the transforming power of the experience.

The challenge of outreach, then, is not to get those on the outside to read, or even to watch others practice. The challenge is rather to get them involved so that they can hear the music and experience the warmth and the richness, to move them to a place where they can feel that their heritage is their own.

Jacob J. Staub
The Jewish Exponent

A HIDDEN TREASURE

The Sabbath is one of those precious heavenly gifts that are given again and again. Many generations have been privileged to receive her as the wise and aged queen, and still to find her new, a radiant bride.

There is no end to the meanings discovered in the Sabbath in every generation; there is no limit to the secrets hidden within this enchanted "sanctuary in time." Even in the Torah itself, the Sabbath is revealed to us from one chapter to another in growing meaning: from a remembrance of Creation to a mark of the Exodus, and an everlasting sign between God and his people. Sabbath is tied to the sanctuary in space as well as to the holiness of the inner mystery of our personal being. The Torah unfolds for us, as if by surprise, ever new ways of translating the command "to sanctify" the day into tangible expression.

The Prophets show us yet other aspects of Sabbath, in letting us into the secret of Sabbath as a delight. It is they who emphasize that, in order to experience its sanctity, we must refrain from indulging in any business transactions. The Rabbis, in their turn, find a thousand new faces of the Sabbath which smile in that enchanted, mysterious way from whatever angle you draw near. They encased the Sabbath in that solid frame of laws... but at the same time they crowned her with the most tender garlands of love and poetry.

They whispered into our ears the secret of the "extra soul" that joins us at the entrance of Sabbath in the luminous rays of the sinking sun on Friday afternoon, and departs from us until the next week, regretfully, in the soft melodious shadows of the Sabbath twilight, to vanish completely with the flame of the *havdalah* candle. They opened our eyes to see the two angels walking at our side as we come home from the synagogue on Friday night and enter our home, transformed into a palace, to greet members of our family, the mother queen, and the princes and princesses around the royal table.

It was the Rabbis who illuminated our homes with the brightness of the Sabbath candles and lit our hearts with the shining hopes of the imminent redemption of which the Sabbath is but a foretaste. It was they who made us wash, change clothing, become different, outwardly as well as inwardly, upon entering the Sabbath. Thus your dress on Sabbath should not be the same as your weekday apparel, your speech on Sabbath should not be as your speech during the week, your thoughts on Sabbath should not be as your thoughts during the week. On Sabbath you are another person, they convinced us, by sharing with us hundreds of minute detailed laws — laws which they hewed from the heavy granite of the mountains of *Halacha*, only to string them lightly on the golden hair of the one they called queen and bride in the *Aggadah*. The laws of Sabbath, they said, are like mountains strung on one hair....

Only God, Israel, the people, Torah, and the land of Israel could be given the same abundance of love and insight bestowed upon the Sabbath in talmudic and midrashic literature. Unable to express everything they wanted to say, the Rabbis resorted to the epitaph — a hidden treasure. With all that can be spoken, more remains hidden, waiting to be unearthed in generations to come.

halacha = Jewish law
aggadah = Jewish legend, story, poetry, tale

Pinhas H. Peli
"Sabbath: A Hasidic Dimension"
From *Perspectives on Jews and Judaism:*
Essays in Honor of Wolfe Kelman

THE SPICE OF THE FEAST

Rabbi Joshua the Prince made a *Shabbat* feast for Emperor Antoninus. Though the food was served cold, it was very good. Some time later, the emperor was the host at a feast. Hot dishes were served. At its conclusion, Antoninus said, "The meal you served was better." Judah said, "This meal lacked a particular spice." The emperor was astonished, "Does my treasury lack anything? Tell me what it is, and it shall be purchased." Judah replied, "*Shabbat* is the spice. It cannot be bought."

Babylonian Talmud, Shabbat 119a

SHABBAT SWEETENS THE WORLD

Yet those who practice the *mitzvot* obtain constant glimpses of eternity. The Jew who takes a cup of wine in his hand on Sabbath eve to praise God as the Creator of all, the Jew who observes the Sabbath in recognition of God's sovereignty does find that, in the words of the Jewish mystics, "the Sabbath sweetens the world." A new dimension is added to his life. However banal and trivial his daily round, on this day he gains insight into ultimate reality. As Abraham Isaac Kuk, the late Chief Rabbi of Palestine said, "just as there are laws of poetry there is poetry in laws."

Louis Jacobs
Great Jewish Ideas

SACRED DUTIES — JOYOUS PERFORMANCE

Uplifting the otherwise dreary life of the Jew in difficult times, conferring meaning and majesty in good times and bad, the Sabbath is the quintessential Jewish institution; for here the ideal of *Simḥah Shel Mitzvah*, the joyous performance of sacred duties, is linked to a rich tapestry of interwoven ceremonies, procedures, liturgies, and creaturely delights.

Max Arzt
Joy and Remembrance

Blessed Is The Home 2

THE ARRIVAL OF THE QUEEN

The Sabbath is a queen whose coming changes the humblest home into a palace.

Babylonian Talmud, Shabbat 119a

A MOTHER'S *SHABBAT* PRAYER
"AS I KINDLE THESE LIGHTS..."

May the light of these candles help inspire us to love You with all our hearts. May their warmth and glow radiate kindness, harmony, and joy among the members of my family; may love and devotion bind us closer to one another and to You. Amen.

Compassionate creator of all life, embrace my life and my family's life with Your lovingkindness. May my children walk in Your ways, loyal to the Torah and adorned with good deeds. Bless our home and our family with peace and light and joy. Amen.

Jules Harlow
Siddur Sim Shalom

THE *SHABBAT* BRINGS GOD NEAR

By the Sabbath every human home and heart recognizes not only the God of the universe, the God of nature, but the God Who is ever near to every human dwelling and heart, under Whose care every dwelling and soul reposes. With this knowledge salvation is brought to every dwelling and peace to every soul. Give the world the Sabbath and you will break the fetters and heal the wounds of mankind.

Samuel H. Dresner
The Sabbath

BE QUICK TO REESTABLISH PEACE

You should be careful on the holy Sabbath to cleave to your fellow man in love and brotherhood, peace and friendship — even more is this true between husband and wife.... So if two people had some dispute they should each one approach the other with words of reconciliation and love before the entrance of *Shabbat.*

Alexander Susskind
Yesod v'Shoresh ha-Avodah

BLESSED IS THE MATCH

Blessed Is The Match
that kindles the Sabbath lights.
Blessed Is The Home
that reflects the glow of the Sabbath Candles

Blessed Is The Heart
that radiates the warmth of the Sabbath peace.

Hannah Senesh
Translation from the United Synagogue Brochure

SABBATH AND THE KITCHEN GIRLS

When an old woman, who had served in her youth in the household of Rabbi Elimelech of Lizensk was asked for stories about the master and his ways, she said:

"During the week, the girls in the kitchen often quarreled, as in other households. But in this we differed from others. On the eve of each Sabbath, we fell around each other's neck, and we begged forgiveness for any harsh words spoken during the week."

I. Berger
"Esser Tzachtzochoth"
in *Hasidic Anthology*

WHOM *SHABBAT* HONORS

One should rise early on Friday to prepare that which is needed for *Shabbos*. Even if one has many servants to serve him, he should strive to prepare (at least) something himself for the *Shabbos*, in order to give the day honor. As we find regarding (the Talmudic Sages): R' Chisda would thinly slice vegetables; Rabbah and R' Yosef would chop wood; R' Zeira would kindle a fire; and R' Nachman would prepare the house by bringing the *Shabbos* vessels in and taking the weekday vessels out. All should take a lesson from these Sages and not say, "Such is beneath my dignity," for through this — giving honor to the *Shabbos* — one is honored.

Joseph Caro
Shulhan Aruh

MAKING *SHABBES*

In Jewish English, the common phrase is *make Shabbes*. It seems logical enough: one person asks another, "Who's making *Shabbes* this week, you or your in-laws?" Immediately, it conjures up images of cooking, cleaning, shopping, organizing, etc. A whole progression of labor is involved in the creation of the day of rest. The idea of *making Shabbes* is a practical concept. It reflects a pragmatic social reality: in order to celebrate a day of rest, someone has to do a lot of work.

The idea of *making Shabbes* is really biblical. The Torah commands the Jewish people to "Guard *Shabbat* — making *Shabbat* throughout their generations" (Exodus 31:17). From the beginning, a Jewish vision of rest had little to do with a recreational use of leisure time. Starting with the beginning of the Torah, rest was defined as a process of RE-CREATION. God spent six days creating. Then the Torah says, ... "God made *Shabbat* and God rested." The word for rest here is *vayinafash*. It is a form of the word *nefesh*, which means "soul." When God rests, the world has soul. When we are commanded to imitate God (living up to the image in which we were created), the expectation is that our rest, too, will be soulful. Creating that kind of rest is something at which we must work.

Ron Wolfson
The Art of Jewish Living — The Shabbat Seder

RICH VALUES OF *SHABBAT*

More Jewish values can be pursued and realized on the Sabbath than on any other day in the calendar. Holiness, worship, study, human freedom and dignity, peace, quiet and contentment, hospitality, spiritual satisfaction together with the moderate and sober enjoyment of material things — these are the rich values to be won from the true and full observance of the Sabbath.

Solomon Goldman
A Guide to the Sabbath

"SHABBAT" INSTEAD OF "SATURDAY"

How nice it would be if "Saturday" would disappear from our vocabulary and "*Shabbat*" would take its place. In the very act of uttering the word *Shabbat* some kind of influence might be exerted over the way we spend the day.

I can't picture, for example, a woman saying, "I am going to the supermarket on *Shabbat*," or "I am doing my laundry on *Shabbat*," I am cooking dinner on *Shabbat*." The incongruity would scream.

Once she uses the word *Shabbat* it would be easier for her to say, "On Friday night we are having our meal, as a family at our *Shabbat* table adorned by candles, *Challot* and wine." "On *Shabbat* morning we are going to services, going to services as a family."

Sidney Greenberg

JUDAISM BEGINS IN THE HOME

Judaism begins in the home. It doesn't begin at a meeting or a conference or at a philanthropic campaign. It begins in homes where Judaism lives in the atmosphere and is integrated in the normal pattern of daily life. It begins in homes where the Jewish words re-echo, where the Jewish book is honored, and the Jewish song is heard. It begins in homes where the child sees and participates in symbols and rites that link him to a people and culture. It begins in homes where the Jewish ceremonial object is visible. It begins in homes where into the deepest layers of a child's developing personality are woven strands of love for and devotion to the life of the Jewish community.

Morris Adler

THE MOTHER'S TEARS

The Jewish world of Lithuania was not one of mystics. But when the twilight shadows fell on the Sabbath Eve, there were moments in each small Lithuanian Jewish town when the entire universe appeared to be standing still, in awe and suspense, awaiting the entry of the Sabbath. In every home the workday week gradually retreated, yielding place to the Sabbath Queen who was about to enter in the glow of the soft Sabbath lights.

Jewish religious life places the woman a little apart from the men, but it was to the woman, the mother of the house, that Judaism entrusted the quiet act of worship which enthrones the Sabbath in the Jewish home, and ah, how superbly did she perform that hallowed task! As her lips gently breathed the blessing over the Sabbath candles, her very soul trembled and set aquiver the spirit that filled her dwelling. That moment, when the mother of the house blessed the Sabbath lights, her hands covering her face, and a tear, perhaps, coursing down her cheek, was one of the most sacred in the Jewish home. What was the reason for the mother's tears at that joyous, festive hour when she brought the Sabbath into her house? The mother standing over the Sabbath lights represented a mute mystery, concealing within herself the secrets of Jewish survival.

Abraham Kariv
Lithuania Of My Birth

A CHOICE

All choices have consequences. If Friday night is going to be time at home, that means turning down invitations for dinner and a movie with friends or family. And for chronically overscheduled people, sitting still for an hour, much less an afternoon, can be a real challenge. However, these are precisely the reasons that many people view *Shabbat* prohibitions less as sacrifices than as opportunities to reorient an overly hectic life around the need for rest, relaxation, and time with family and close friends.

Diamant & Cooper
Living a Jewish Life

RESTORATIVE MAGIC

The Sabbath has cut most sharply athwart my own life when one of my plays has been in rehearsal or in tryout. The crisis atmosphere of an attempt at Broadway is a legend of our time, and a true one; I have felt under less pressure going into battle at sea. Friday afternoon, during these rehearsals, inevitably seems to come when the project is tottering on the edge of ruin. I have sometimes felt guilty of treason, holding to the Sabbath in such a desperate situation. But then, experience has taught me that a theatre enterprise almost always is in such a case. Sometimes it does totter to ruin, and sometimes it totters to great prosperity, but tottering is its normal gait, and cries of anguish are its normal tone of voice. So I have reluctantly taken leave of my colleagues on Friday afternoon, and rejoined them on Saturday night. The play has never yet collapsed in the meantime. When I return I find it tottering as before, and the anguished cries as normally despairing as ever. My plays have encountered in the end both success and failure, but I cannot honestly ascribe either result to my observing the Sabbath.

Leaving the gloomy theatre, the littered coffee cups, the jumbled scarred-up scripts, the haggard actors, the shouting stagehands, the bedeviled director, the knuckle-gnawing producer, the clattering typewriter, and the dense tobacco smoke and backstage dust, I have come home. It has been a startling change, very like a brief return from the wars. My wife and my boys, whose existence I have almost forgotten in the anxious shoring up of the tottering ruin, are waiting for me, gay, dressed in holiday clothes, and looking to me marvelously attractive. We have sat down to a splendid dinner, at a table graced with flowers and the old Sabbath symbols: the burning candles, the twisted loaves, the stuffed fish, and my grandfather's silver goblet brimming with wine. I have blessed my boys with the ancient blessing; we have sung the pleasantly syncopated Sabbath table hymns. The talk has had little to do with tottering ruins. My wife and I have caught up with our week's conversation. The boys, knowing that the Sabbath is the occasion for asking questions have asked them. The Bible, the encyclopedia, the atlas, have piled up on the table. We talk of Judaism, and there are the usual impossible boys' queries about God, which my wife and I field clumsily but as well as we can. For me it is a retreat into restorative magic.

Herman Wouk
This Is My God

THE BINDING GLUE FOR THE FAMILY

I recently came across an interview with Gary Gene Allen and Karen Lawrence Allen, a husband and wife team of human-resource development consultants in Washington, D.C. They are authors of *Roots and Wings: Discovering and Developing Family Strengths.*

The Allens were asked for suggestions to promote family cohesion at a time when there is too much family fragmentation. Here are some of their suggestions for strengthening the family:

1) "No matter how hectic their schedules, family members must stay intimately involved in each other's lives. Parents must make time to talk to their kids about the details of their daily lives, even if it means making compromises in their careers or elsewhere in their lives."

2) "Develop strong family rituals and tradition. Besides providing important opportunities for shared fun, these help foster a sense of continuity from one generation to the next."

3) "Find activities the whole family can enjoy. Our culture tends to segregate people according to age, with adults going one way and children another. Given this arrangement, it's all too easy for family members of one generation to fall out of sync with those of another. To stay in sync, spend time together."

Why do I feel impelled to share their suggestions with all of us? I do so in the firm belief that each of their suggestions which I have quoted constitutes a compelling argument for *Shabbat* observance.

They urge us to set aside time for family members to "catch up" with one another. Isn't the *Shabbat* meal a wonderful opportunity for the family to do just that? In a relaxed unhurried atmosphere we have time to talk to one another and to listen to one another.

The Allens further suggest that we "develop strong family rituals and traditions." We Jews don't have to create new rituals and traditions. We have a sublime collection of Sabbath rituals and traditions. What wonderful bonding they can create between the members of the family and the larger Jewish family, past and present.

Listen to how Elie Wiesel remembers the *Shabbat* of his childhood. "I shall never forget *Shabbat* in my town. When I shall have forgotten everything else, my memory will still retain the atmosphere of holiday, of serenity pervading even the poorest houses; the white tablecloth, the candles, the meticulously combed little girls, the men on their way to the synagogue. When my town shall fade into the abyss of time, I will continue to remember the light and the warmth it radiated on *Shabbat*. As it enveloped the universe, the *Shabbat* conferred on it a dimension of peace, an aura of love."

The Allens further suggest that we "find activities the whole family can enjoy." The family *Shabbat* observance is a ready made vehicle for precisely such an activity. In his recent book, *To Life*, my friend and colleague Harold Kushner talks about the contribution that *Shabbat* can make to the joy of family living. "The ceremony of welcoming the Sabbath is one of the most magical moments in all of Judaism. When I speak to young couples about to be married about how to fill their home with Jewishness, when I talk to people searching for something to do differently to fill the spiritual vacuum in their souls, when young parents ask me how they can give their children more of a religious upbringing than they themselves had, the Friday night rituals of welcoming the Sabbath are the first things I recommend. They work their magic even on people who are ordinarily not given to religious ritual."

If ever a generation needed the binding glue of *Shabbat* ours is that generation. A precious legacy has been handed to us. Let us take full advantage of it. Our lives will be so much richer when we do.

Sidney Greenberg

WE MUST CONVERT SATURDAY TO *SHABBAT*

The biblical phrase which we translate "to observe the Sabbath" is literally translated "to make the Sabbath." The Yiddish phrase, "*Machen Shabbos*," conveys better the meaning of the Hebrew words. It is we who must make the Sabbath, it is we who must convert Saturday to *Shabbat*, it is we who must prepare for it, welcome it, and celebrate its special sacred character. Only then can we recognize the preciousness of the gift God gave us when He sanctified the day on which He rested from His work of creation.

Sidney Greenberg

TZEDAKAH — A JEWISH PASSION

Tzedakah, the obligation to share one's resources to help others in need, is a Jewish passion. Jews have ingeniously woven the giving of *tzedakah* into the celebration of every holiday and every *simha* (joyous event). In the case of *Shabbat*, wherein the handling of money is prohibited, it became a practice to make the giving of *tzedakah* the culmination of preparation for the holiday. It is a common practice to drop a few coins in a *tzedakah* box just before lighting the candles. This can be done with the ubiquitous Jewish National Fund "blue box," an object d'art crafted especially for this purpose, a canister your children made in religious school, or even an old jar. In some families it has become a practice to include a discussion of how these *tzedakah* funds should be utilized.

Ron Wolfson
The Art of Jewish Living — The Shabbat Seder

A CHANCE TRULY TO REST

Almighty God,
Grant me and all my loved ones
A Chance truly for rest on this *Shabbat*.
May the light of the candles drive out from among us
The spirit of anger, the spirit of harm.
Send your blessings to my children,
That they may walk in the ways of your Torah, your light.

Translated from the Yiddish by Arthur Green
in *The Jewish Catalog*
by Michael Strassfeld and Richard Seigel

EVERY JEW — A SPIRITUAL PRODIGY

At the Friday night *Shabbat* meal, Jewish parents bless their children in the following manner: to sons they say, "may you be like Ephraim and Menashe," and to daughters they say, "may you be like Sarah, Rebecca, Rachel and Leah." With this blessing we do not request that our children become another Sarah or Ephraim, rather that they may similarly become inspirational in their spirit, moral fiber and strength of character. Every Jewish child has the potential to reach new heights by putting forth their best efforts towards an expression of unlimited possibilities.

HOW DOES WINE BECOME INVOLVED IN THE *KIDDUSH*?

Because *Shabbat* is associated with *joy* ("You shall call the Sabbath a joy," Isaiah 58:13) and because wine is also understood in Jewish tradition to be a symbol of joy ("Wine makes *glad* the human heart," Psalms 104:15), the Rabbis declared that *Shabbat* should be sanctified using wine. It is important to note that the *Kiddush* is not a prayer in which the wine is sanctified. Rather, it is a prayer in which the wine is used in order to sanctify *Shabbat*.

If you do not have wine, you may omit the blessing, "... *borei peri hagafen*." Instead, recite the *Motsi* over bread followed by the *Kiddush* paragraph which sanctifies *Shabbat*.

Gates of Shabbat

WHY IS THE *CHALLAH* COVERED UNTIL THE *MOTZI*

Since bread is a basic part of almost every meal, some people keep the *challah* out of sight in order to highlight the Friday evening ceremonies of candlelighting and *Kiddush*. Once it is clear that the meal is not an ordinary one but in honor of *Shabbat,* the *challah* is uncovered and the *Motzi* is recited.

Another explanation for this custom is based on the *challah's* symbolic representation of the manna. The cover over the *challah* and the plate or platter which is usually placed underneath the *challah* are said to represent the two layers of dew between which the manna fell, protecting it from the sand of the Sinai desert below and the heat of the sun above.

A popular explanation for children is that the *challah* is covered in order not to embarrass the bread when the candles and wine are dealt with first. When covering the *challah* on your table, a napkin can suffice. You can also purchase or even make special *challah* covers to add to the beauty of your evening.

Gates of Shabbat

WHY ARE TWO LOAVES USED?

The two loaves represent the double share of manna which, according to the Torah (Exodus 16:22), fell each Friday in order to feed our ancestors on their journey from Egypt to Canaan. Collecting the double portion of manna on Friday meant that the Israelites did not have to collect food when *Shabbat* arrived.

Gates of Shabbat

A Sign Forever   *3*

SABBATH — A SIGN OF ETERNITY

The Torah calls *Shabbos* (*Ex.* 31:17), "an eternal sign." The author of *Reshis Chochmah* writes that this means that it is a "sign of Eternity." On *Shabbos*, the door opens a crack, and we see a spark of the Eternal. We feel a breeze blowing from the Future World when all is Sabbath. The *Shabbos* feeling is a sign of the Future, when man and God will be in total harmony.

Aryeh Kaplan
Sabbath Day of Eternity

A DAY SPEAKS OF SOMETHING ETERNAL

The Sabbath does not mean a mere not working, nor an empty idleness. It connotes something positive. It has guided the soul unto its mystery, so that it is not a day that just interrupts, but a day that renews, speaks through it, of something eternal. It is the expression of a direction for life and not just an instituted day of rest. If it were only that, or if it became that, its essence would be taken from it. It would then be only a hollow shell.

Leo Baeck
The Essence of Judaism

ON A CLEAR *SHABBAT* YOU CAN SEE FOREVER

As human beings we live under the tyranny of time. Time dictates so much of what we do, when we do it, and the pace at which we do it. Is time a friend or a foe? It depends on how we use it.

We can do many things with time. We can kill it. We can waste it. The speeding motorist "makes" time. The prisoner "serves" time. The referee "calls" time. But time, as Benjamin Franklin reminded us, "is the stuff life is made of."

But human beings also inhabit a world beyond time. Unhurried, unhassled, and unbattered by the people and events that make claims upon our time, we are given a day to put time on a shelf and to be timeless. I mean the *Shabbat*, of course, which the Torah declares an *ot*, a sign — a sign of the timeless.

"The Israelites shall keep *Shabbat*," God says. "It shall be a sign for all time between me and the people of Israel" (Ex. 32:16-17).

People who live only by the signs of the time have no taste of the timeless. Buffeted about by the winds of change, they know nothing of the eternal. Perhaps the most typical sign of our time is the list we all carry, in our head or on paper, of things to get done before night falls, so that we can crawl wearily into bed and start a new list the next morning. *Shabbat* is a day without lists, a day when nothing has to get done.

Shabbat is a sign of the timeless in a more profound respect as well. It is a weekly reminder of the presence of people in our lives.

There are the relationships that matter which do not depend on the times: the love between parents and children, perhaps, or the timelessness of a moment you share with the person who knows you better than you know yourself. These things surpass the limited scope of our daily listmaking. In the timelessness of *Shabbat*, we are invited to celebrate the miracle of other people with whom we take "time out" from time, that we and they may sanctify *Shabbat* together.

Last, the timelessness of *Shabbat* convinces us that God is real. The Chafetz Chaim contrasted the sign of *Shabbat* with the temporary signs on storefronts or office buildings. We may arrive to find the entrances locked and the lights out. But the presence of the signs testify to the fact that the storekeeper or the doctor must be out only temporarily. The store or office will reopen tomorrow, or after lunch, or in an hour. But if we find the sign taken down, we know the owner or doctor has irrevocably moved, probably never to be seen again.

God, too, seems to be absent much of the time. In moments of distress we have no guarantee that God will be present to us, just as we do not know for sure that the doctor will be in or the store will be open. But *Shabbat* is a sign that God has not vanished forever, a sign that God is available, though perhaps not immediately, not now, not at our beck and call — as long a Jews keep *Shabbat*, that is!

The moment we lose *Shabbat*, the sign of the timeless is, as it were, taken down. Lost in the mire of the times alone, we may then be doomed to them as well.

"Those who do not keep *Shabbat* shall surely die," says our Torah. Not "they shall be put to death." No, they will simply die; they will die the spiritual death of those who have lost the ability to see beyond the times.

For those who keep *Shabbat*, on the other hand, God becomes a palpable presence. It's really true; on a clear *Shabbat*, you can see forever.

Lawrence A. Hoffman
The Jewish Week

CONSECRATION OF YOURSELF TO GOD

Issur melakhah — "abstinence from work," this is the sign which your God expects from you on every Sabbath. Abstinence from work is the sign which He seeks to prove whether you can still call yourself His. Abstinence from work is the sign by which you are to demonstrate that God is the Creator of heaven and earth, that He is also your Creator and that you, too, belong to Him.

For six days the world belongs to you, for six days you may exercise your dominion over everything that your God has created, and perform "*melakhah*;" you may stamp your creative impression upon everything and make it the agent of your will, the executor of your purpose. But on the seventh day you shall testify that, after all, the world is not yours, that you are not its ultimate ruler, but merely God's vassal on earth, that you live and work only by God's grace, that He is your Lord and Master, the Lord and Master of the smallest as of the greatest creature within your ken. To this you shall testify by giving the world its freedom on this day, by retiring into that sphere which is subject to you and by not exerting your powers on any work of God to bend it to your purpose.

By *issur melakhah*, by abstinence from work on the Sabbath, you place yourself and your work reverently on God's holy altar.

By *issur melakhah* you make the twenty-four hours of the Sabbath a continual dedication of the world to your God and a consecration of yourself.

Pinhas H. Peli
The Jewish Sabbath

SYMBOL OF OUR HIGHER DESTINY

The Sabbath is the day of rest, the consecrated covenant between God
and Man. It is much more than mere relaxation from labor. It is a sign
and symbol of man's higher destiny. We must say to ourselves, "So far
shall I go in my pursuit of things of life and no further. Beyond that I
am a free man, a child of God. Beyond that I have a soul and I must
give to it time, energy and interest.

Abba Hillel Silver
"Leisure and the Church"
in *Religion in a Changing World*

THE CORNERSTONE OF JUDAISM

I wish to explain the concept of *Oneg Shabbat*. We are coming to *Eretz*
Israel to renew our life, to create for ourselves a distinctive life, with
features and characteristics uniquely our own. And in order to create
forms of life that are rooted and genuine, that are true to the character
of the nation, the founders of the *Oneg Shabbat* movement felt that
they must use for their creative work only such material as is derived
from the foundation stones of the original forms of life. They felt that
they must dig down to the strongest of all foundations, to the very
cornerstone of Jewish life. And in their search they found no form
loftier or more profound than the Sabbath, which preceded the giving
of the Torah and was observed by the Children of Israel while they
were still in Egypt. The Sabbath is indeed the cornerstone of Judaism,
and it is not without cause that it is called the "sign of the covenant"
between God and the children of Israel. In the Sabbath are enfolded
many national and social concepts. If in the Ten Commandments is
enfolded the whole Torah, then in the Sabbath are probably enfolded
all the Ten Commandments.

Hayyim Nahman Bialik
Sefer Ha-Shabbat

KEEP AS MUCH OF THE SABBATH AS YOU ARE ABLE

When dire necessity compels a Jew to break the Sabbath, let him not think that the Sabbath is lost to him, or he to Judaism. So long as Jewish conscientiousness is alive within him, let him endeavor to keep as much of the Sabbath as he is able. He must not say, "I have broken the Sabbath. How can I join my brethren in the Sabbath Service!" Whatever he does conscientiously will be acceptable before God, and he will thus find himself exhorted to watch carefully, and to seize the first opportunity of returning to the full observance of Sabbath.

M. Friedlander

ISRAEL'S MATE

When the world was created, *Shabbat* said to the Holy One, "Ruler of the Universe, every living thing created has its mate, and each day has its companion, except me, the seventh day. I am alone!" God answered, "The people of Israel will be your mate."

When the Israelites arrived at Mount Sinai, the Holy One said to them, "Remember what I said to *Shabbat* — that the people of Israel would be her mate?" It is with reference to this that My fourth commandment for you reads: "*Remember* the Sabbath day, to keep it holy."

Genesis Rabbah 11:8

A LITMUS TEST OF JEWISH LOYALTY

The Sabbath is designated in the Bible as the sign of the ongoing covenant, or agreement, between God and Israel. It is, in other words, the
expression of the whole relationship between God and Israel, and most
especially of the bond of the People Israel to all of God's laws. Just as
tefillin are a reminder of all of God's commandments, so the Sabbath is.
For that reason we do not put on *tefillin* on the Sabbath: *Shabbat* itself
is a sign of the commandments, and we therefore need no other symbol on that day. For the same reason the Rabbis declare the Sabbath to
be the equivalent of all the other *mitzvot*, and the prophet Ezekiel
repeatedly singles out the Sabbath as the litmus test of the extent to
which Israel was observing God's law and the strength or weakness of
the whole relationship between God and Israel.

Elliot N. Dorff
Knowing God: Jewish Journeys to the Unknowable

THE GREAT EDUCATOR

Religious worship and religious instruction — the renewal of man's
spiritual life in God — form an essential part of Sabbath observance.
We, therefore, sanctify the Sabbath by a special Sabbath liturgy, by
statutory lessons from the Torah and the Prophets, and by attention to
discourse and instruction by religious teachers. The Sabbath has thus
proved the great educator in Israel in the highest education of all, namely,
the laws governing human conduct. The effect of the Sabbath prayers
and synagogue homilies upon the Jewish people have been incalcu-
lable. Leopold Zunz... has shown that almost the whole of Israel's
inner history since the close of Bible times can be traced in following
the development of these Sabbath discourses on the Torah. Sabbath
worship is still the chief bond which unites Jews into a religious brotherhood.

Joseph H. Hertz
Pentateuch and Haftorahs

A Day of Delight and Joy *4*

HOW TO EXPRESS JOY

The Prophet Isaiah says, "And you shall call the Sabbath a delight."
How does a person express joy on *Shabbat?* By eating even the smallest amount of food as long as it is prepared in honor of *Shabbat.*

Babylonian Talmud Shabbat 118b

THE WHOLE PERSON SERVES GOD

One celebrates the day not only by meditation and prayer, but also by
wearing Sabbath clothes and by partaking of the Sabbath meals. The
Sabbath meal itself is a *mitzvah*; it is a divine service. And if properly
performed, it is a service of a far higher quality than that of prayer and
meditation alone; it is the service of the whole man.

The enjoyment of the Sabbath is neither spiritual nor material; it is
wholly human. Body and spirit celebrate the Sabbath in communion.
The Jew who keeps the Sabbath may say that the material enjoyments
of the day enhance his spiritual elation and that his spiritual elation
renders the material enjoyments more gratifying. In the unifying act of
the *mitzvah* the Sabbath acts as "a spice" to the palate and as an exhila-
rating joy for the spirit of man.

Eliezer Berkovits
God, Man and History

A TASTE OF PERFECTION

Joy is a foretaste of the world to come. It is a hint of the mode of being in which humans and God are in perfect relationship with one another.

In this life, one can only know joy in relationship with another person. From the wisdom of the Jewish imagination and its revelatory tradition has come practical responses to the necessity of joy in this life in order to sustain our faith in the life beyond death.

Foremost among these responses is the Sabbath, which is the model for prophecy in this world. God and humans draw near to one another in the imagination, where the prophet hears the voice of God and finds the language with which to express what he has heard for others. This is the revelatory tradition.

The Sabbath is the Jewish assertion that these two worlds can become one. On the Sabbath, we are freed from the constraints of worldly cares; we act as though we live in redeemed time. This is a breathtaking act of imaginative daring and, ideally, requires the concerted effort of the entire community of Israel to work. Each Jew who does not participate in this effort removes one layer of imaginative film from the experience of the whole. If enough people do not participate, it becomes impossible for those who do to feel the imaginative actuality of the world-to-come. On the other hand, joining together in an imaginative relationship of all of Israel can be so powerful as to effect not only a taste of the world-to-come, but also its advent.

Shabbat, therefore, provides those who observe it with the faith necessary to pursue the perfection needed to bring redemption by letting them taste its fruits each week. At the same time, it provides the environment for the prophetic experience itself — the experience of imaginative speculation — which is necessary for the pursuit of perfection. Finally, within each *Shabbat* is the power to bring on the ideal future whenever humans are collectively ready for it.

May we live to see such perfection in our own time.

Ira F. Stone
Seeking the Path to Life

WE ARE CO-SANCTIFIERS

While Judaism loves life and the pleasure of life, it retains its sobriety by remembering the ambitions and responsibilities of Jewish life — to sanctify the uncompleted world. God is *asher kiddeshanu* — He Who has sanctified us so that we may in turn sanctify the world. We are co-sanctifiers. Who would extinguish the power to bless by deliberately obliterating human awareness? Drunkenness is an injury to the self, a neglect of the world, and an insult to the Creator. We who prepare the wine, that makes the hearts of men and women to sing, remain sober so that we may rejoice the inhabitants who dwell in God's world.

Harold M. Schulweis
In God's Mirror

THE RESERVOIR THE SABBATH HOLDS

When the prosecutor at my trial in Moscow railed against Israel, he said, "It is a terrible place ruled by *Shabbat*, with its twenty-four hours of silent mourning." In his diatribe, *Shabbat* became an all-encompassing term, conjuring ancient rites, primitive forces born of superstition and ignorance, medieval relics, the peculiar customs of the "elders."

He did not grasp the meaning — the reservoir of wisdom, joy, harmony and warmth — that *Shabbat* holds.

Natan Sharansky

WHAT THE PURITANS DID NOT KNOW

To the Jews the Sabbath is a day of happiness. The synagogue liturgy of the Sabbath is full of the joyous note. It is marked by gay dress, sumptuous meals, and a general sense of exhilaration. The Puritans knew little or nothing of synagogue worship or of Jewish homes. They had no experience of "the joy of the commandment" — a phrase often on Jewish lips and in Jewish hearts.

William Selbie
Influence of Old Testament on Puritanism

TO LIVE, TO EAT, TO ENJOY

The "work" that is forbidden by Jewish law on the Sabbath is not measured in the expenditure of energy. It takes real effort to pray, to study, to walk to synagogue. They are "rest" but not restful. Forbidden "work" is acquisition, aggrandizement, altering the world. On *Shabbat* we are obliged to be, to reflect, to love and make love, to eat, to enjoy.

Arnold Jacob Wolf
Gates of *Shabbat*

HOW LONG IS A WEEK?

One man complained that a week is the shortest distance between two Mondays and the longest distance between two pay days.

For the Jew who loves *Shabbat* and delights in all the physical and spiritual gifts it brings in such marvelous abundance, a week is too long a distance between two Sabbaths.

Sidney Greenberg

AN EXQUISITE SHARING WITH THOSE WE LOVE

Shabbat is an extended meditation on the wonders of the created world and the divine presence that fills it. The weekly stopping of the clock and relief from all pressures and obligations of the workday world, from the ongoing demand to recreate and transform reality, is needed more than ever in our fast-paced world. It gives us the opportunity to enjoy the world as we have received it and to bask in its holy light. *Shabbat* is, if you will, contemplation turned into a way of living. Rather than the one and silent contemplative act, which lies at the heart of all prayer, *Shabbat* is that same contemplation turned into the mode of family and communal joy and celebration. In its ideal form, it is an exquisite sharing with those we love of our awareness that we, the world around us, and that love itself, are all gifts from the one source of life.

This is not the place to elaborate on precisely how the Sabbath should be celebrated. Ultimately, it should be a day of joy and not restriction. The rules for *Shabbat* exist in order to create the sacred time in which the transformation of consciousness that is *Shabbat's* real meaning may take place. This observer has found that many of the larger rules make sense. Avoidance of travel, of commerce, and of all forms of schedule watching and weekday obligation seem to lie at the core of the *Shabbat* experience. The finer details of *Shabbat* observance will have to be tried and tested by each seeker or community. Some will do better with more of the traditional *halakhah*, others with less, depending largely on individual needs for structure or freedom. But some sort of halakhic form should be firmly established, for it is this that creates the needed "fence" within which *Shabbat* consciousness can live.

Arthur Green
Seek My Face, Speak My Name

DAY OF DELIGHT

In addition to "remembering" and "keeping" the Sabbath, the Rabbis derive further Sabbath ideas from the verse in the Book of Isaiah (58:3): "If thou turn away your foot because of the Sabbath, from pursuing thy business on My holy day; And call the Sabbath a delight; And the holy of the Lord honorable, And shall honor it, not doing your wonted ways; Not pursuing thy business; nor speaking thereof." The two basic ideas derived from the verse are: *Oneg Shabbat* ("Sabbath delight") and *Kavod Shabbat* ("Sabbath honor," paying special honor to the day). The Sabbath is to be treated as a day of delight (in this context, quiet enjoyment) and a day to be welcomed and treated as an honored guest. Jews wear special Sabbath clothes ("the Sabbath best"); eat special meals (one on Friday night and two during the day); walk tranquilly and unhurriedly (unless one enjoys running as sport); take time for prayer and for study of the Torah; spend time with one's family; banish care and worry so far as possible; and bathe on the eve of the Sabbath so as to enter the Sabbath well-groomed. In furtherance of these ideas, cheerful songs — *zemirot* — are sung at the Sabbath table.

Louis Jacobs
The Book of Jewish Practices

WE MUST PREPARE FOR THE SABBATH

"Remember the Sabbath day, to keep it holy" (Ex. 20:8). But is one liable to forget the Sabbath day? For it does recur every seventh day. The verse means to imply that one must remember to remove those things which would make him forget to remember the Sabbath. For example, one should not be sad on the Sabbath.... Each Sabbath, one should do those things which remind him that it is Sabbath: One should bathe on Sabbath eve and dress in his best clothes and arrange for an *Oneg Shabbat* ("joy of the Sabbath") celebration, and read those things which are suitable for the Sabbath day....

"On the sixth day they shall prepare" (Ex. 16:5). One must very diligently prepare for the Sabbath in advance. He must be diligent and quick in this as one who has heard that the Queen is going to lodge at his home, or as one who has heard that a bride and all her company are coming to his home. What would he do in such instances? He would greatly rejoice and say: "They do me great honor by staying under my roof." He would say to his servants: "Make the house ready, set it in order, sweep it out and make the beds in honor of those who are coming. I shall go to buy as much bread, meat and fish as I can, in their honor."

What, for us, is greater than the Sabbath? The Sabbath is a bride, a Queen; the Sabbath is called a delight. Therefore, we surely must take pains to prepare for the Sabbath; each person himself must prepare, even though he has one hundred servants.

Judah the Pious
The Book of the Pious

A BIT OF *SHABBAT* IN EACH DAY

In the Torah we are commanded "You shall keep my Sabbaths (Exodus 31:13). We would expect the text to read "You shall keep my Sabbath" — singular. Why Sabbaths — plural?

The text seems to teach us that we do not confine the Sabbath to one day of the week. Indeed, we refer to days of the week as "the first day of the Sabbath," "the second day of the Sabbath," and so on. Each day of the week should have a portion of *Shabbat* in it. The love and the uplift that we experience on *Shabbat* should flavor and elevate every day of the week.

Elimelech of Lizensk
Noam Elimelech

HENRIETTA SZOLD'S STRENGTH

Henrietta Szold's usual working day went from 4:30 AM until midnight. When she was once asked what was the source of her strength and endurance, she answered: "There are two reasons; one, I keep the Sabbath; and two, my cast-iron stomach."

She went on to explain that when she lit her *Shabbat* candles, she set aside all concerns, and turned toward the delight of the Sabbath, renewing her strength for the work of the coming week.

Sidney Greenberg

The Sabbath is a mirror of the world to come.

Zohar, Genesis, 48a

IT MAY SAVE US FROM THE TRIVIAL

I believe that room for *Shabbos* must be found within our own souls, if we are to survive. It cannot be brought through preaching. The threat of fire and brimstone will not bring receptivity to it. Instead we must get up one day and begin to ask ourselves why, indeed, God created us and for what reason were we sent to the world? *Shabbos* is for me that day dedicated to a pondering of that question. *Shabbos* is set aside for a turning back into ourselves within the synagogue and within the inner circle of family. *Shabbos* is the joy and affirmation that must come when we withdraw from a world of clatter back into ourselves and into real contact with those we love, a day that is only theirs and ours, a day of being not becoming.

In short, *Shabbos* is a dimension in our lives that may yet save us from the meaningless and trivial, from the irrelevant and senseless that crowds our minds and perverts our lives, if only our hearts are open enough and our spirits strong and vital enough.

                                                        Alexander M. Shapiro

A MESSIANIC CELEBRATION

Every Sabbath is a Messianic celebration. For twenty-four hours a fore-taste of the Messianic kingdom is savored by the Jew in peace and security and spiritual concentration. If at its end the Messiah still has not come Jews conclude it with pleading songs invoking at least his herald the prophet Elijah. The Messianic calendar could be continued indefinitely, for literally every single day in the year is suffused with Messianic expectations, prayers and preparations: fifty days lead from the Messianic Passover to the Messianic Feast of Weeks — and every day may turn out to be the last before the advent: never ask on what day the bell tolls; it tolls today. This is the meaning of the phrase which we quoted at the outset from Maimonides: "he may come on any day."

                                                        Steven S. Schwarzschild
                                                        Great Jewish Ideas

A WEEKLY TRUCE

The Sabbath offers a weekly truce, one day in seven when we pause in our struggle with the world, when we stop trying to change it or improve upon it, when we stop even our competition with our others in the sphere of getting and spending. We rest on the Sabbath, not out of exhaustion, and not because we have accomplished everything we wanted to, but because we want to remind ourselves of what it feels like to be at peace with the world. The Rabbis called the Sabbath "a foretaste of the world to come," a sample of what life will be like when it will be good enough so that we no longer have to struggle with it to change it.

Harold Kushner

LEARN BY LIVING IT

The Sabbath is more than a mere set of rules. It is another way of life completely, totally divorced from weekday life. When put in handbook form, a different life style may seem very difficult and complex. When lived, however, it is really very easy.

A good example is going off to college. Every university prints a catalog, telling of all its rules and regulations and including a list of courses. If your sole impression of campus life were to be based on this catalog, it would seem impossibly complicated. After all, it takes a 200-page book just to describe it! But once you get there, you learn to live it.

The same is true of *Shabbos*. You learn to keep the Sabbath by reading books, but that makes it seem impossibly difficult. It is almost like learning about love from a marriage manual. You have to live it to see its true dimensions of beauty.

Aryeh Kaplan
Sabbath Day of Eternity

MAKING *SHABBAT* SPECIAL

It there is one institution that has been consistently cherished by the Jewish people throughout our history, it has been the Sabbath. In the Talmudic tractate of *Shabbat* (119a), we read that the Roman Emperor Hadrian asked, "Why is it that the Sabbath food has such a fragrant scent?" Rabbi Joshua answered, "We put in a certain spice called *Shabbat.*" The Emperor said, "Please give me some of that spice." Rabbi Joshua answered, "It is effective only for those who keep the *Shabbat.*"

Over the years, rather than focusing on the pleasures of the Sabbath and the joy of observing that special day, many in the Jewish community have come to see *Shabbat* as a burden. Some see it as an interruption of the weekly cycle — others as impinging on their personal freedom. Further, the Jewish community has focused much attention on the prohibitions associated with this most treasured day. While these prohibitions are important, many positive precepts can be instituted to help strengthen one's commitment to *Shabbat.*

1) Before *Shabbat* begins, give *tzedakah.* Each member of the family can make a personal contribution to the family *pushke*, and thus play a part in building a better world. By adding "spice" to the life of another, you can add richness to your *Shabbat* experience.

2) Make the house special. Put flowers on the table. Use a special tablecloth and dishes. Make *Shabbat* feel different.

3) Light the *Shabbat* candles. This brief act of ushering in the Sabbath in the presence of loved ones adds glow to this special day and makes the house into a home.

4) Have a special *Shabbat* meal with a brief home service. Make sure the entire family is together. Invite special guests and prepare your favorite dishes.

5) Make *Shabbat* a day to reconnect. Share something significant that happened during the week. Listen to what others have to say.

6) Learn! *Shabbat* is traditionally a time for study. Acquire knowledge other than that needed for school or work.

7) Attend services at your synagogue. Pray. *Shabbat* gives us an opportunity to strengthen our relationship with God. Regular synagogue attendance strengthens our familiarity with the act of praying, making it easier to communicate with God. It also binds us to the rest of the Jewish community.

8) Provide a special treat for *Shabbat*. One week, make it a special snack. At another time, let it be a special book or magazine.

9) Share *Shabbat* with friends. Too often, we don't have the time to let our friends know that we care. Spend time talking, walking and being together.

10) Find special activities that will allow you to interact. By planning an activity that you can do with others, you strengthen the connections between you.

11) Think. Reevaluate your life. Take inventory. Reflect on the week that was. We can thus relive the pleasant moments, making them last longer. Also, by reflecting on our lives, we can plan the next week to ensure greater chances for personal growth.

12) Recite *Havdalah*. Conclude *Shabbat* with the brief, meaningful service over the wine, the spices and the light.

Shabbat is a beautiful day. But the beauty is lost unless it is experienced. Let us each take steps to enrich our *Shabbat* and help to preserve Judaism through personal Jewish living.

Jerome M. Epstein
United Synagogue Review

THE JOYS OF *SHABBAT*

We give thanks on *Shabbat* for our capacity to feel joy, and for the many sources of joy which You have lavished upon us:

The joy of *Shabbat*, day of rest and renewal, and the joy of being reminded that You created us in love;

The joy of *Shabbat* prayer which enables us to reach up to You, to reach out to one another, and to reach deep into ourselves;

The joy of *Shabbat* food and drink, of love — physical and spiritual — of music and poetry and beauty;

The joy of performing *Mitzvot*, and of bringing joy to others through acts of lovingkindness;

The joy of studying and growing through Torah, of touching the life-giving source of our people's spiritual strength.

For these joys which we share, we give thanks, as we seek to fulfill the words of the Psalmist:

> "Worship the Lord in gladness,
> Come into His presence with sounds of joy!"

Sidney Greenberg
Siddur Hadash

TO DRINK LIFE DEEPLY

The commandment to bless this wine is a commandment to drink life
as deeply as we drink from this cup.

It is a commandment to bless life and to love deeply.

It is a commandment to remember with *Shabbat* heart,
to act with *Shabbat* hands,
to see the world with *Shabbat* eyes.

It is a commandment to laugh until we are all laughter,
to sing until we are all song,
to dance until we are all dance,
to love until we are all love.

This is the wine that God has commanded us to bless and drink.

Sandy Eisenberg Sasso
Kol Haneshamah

A BLESSING IN ITSELF

Families with young children can find *Shabbat* observance and commandments a source for concentrating energies on the family as a whole.
Friday night dinner or *Shabbat* lunch might be the ideal opportunity to
allow each child to show off what he or she has learned during the
week. We often do not have the time to see what was learned at ballet,
or hear the new songs from the nursery school. Gathered around the
Shabbat table, each individual can be the focus of leisurely attention.

Walks to synagogue or around the neighborhood on a beautiful *Shabbat* day; sitting around the table singing, or talking, or learning together; inviting friends to share some of our special time away from the
weekday pace — all these times and more build a structure and feel for
a day that one has to experience in order to understand.

Jane Epstein
"Experience Shabbat"
Your Child

OUR PART OF THE BARGAIN

One of the best bulletin columns I ever read is by my colleague, Rabbi Charles Shalman. In that column he talks about worshippers who display in their shirt pockets, their pens and pencils at *Shabbat* (and Festival) services. According to Jewish practice, objects use for actions prohibited on *Shabbat*, such as pens used for writing, are to be put away. Rabbi Shalman writes:

"We need visual symbols and rituals to concretize the concepts that we cannot see. Just as we light candles to illuminate the boundary between workday and Holy Day, we also need a gesture for putting aside the cares of the office when we enter the *Shabbat*.

The institution of the Jewish Sabbath, its nature, its development and its law, is the hardest thing in all of Judaism to explain to Gentiles and is just as difficult to explain to many Jews, who were never exposed to it or who rebelled against a caricature of it.

The only way to describe the laws of the Sabbath is to say that they are a marvelous spiritual structure, built on the foundation of the words of the Bible by master craftsmen of Torah who accepted the mandate of God to apply Torah to life. As the great Frankfort rabbi, Samson Raphael Hirsch, observed in the last century: "The Jewish child who refrains from catching the butterfly or plucking the flower on the Sabbath glorifies the Almighty God more effectively than the most brilliant orators and poets glorify Him by their words and songs." And this is very true, as well, of the Jewish adult who puts aside pen or computer, money, and the workday materials, in honor of *Shabbat*."

The only way that we can appreciate the Classical Jewish Sabbath is by observing it -- or at least studying about it, approaching it with an open mind and soul. Conservative Judaism teaches that while there may be legitimate reinterpretation of Sabbath Law to enhance Shabbat observance, the structure of the Classical Shabbat is very much an essential pillar of Jewish life, one of the ways that we Jews bring a foretaste of Divine redemption into our lives and into the world. Now, as in ages past, we have the power and the mandate to make the Sabbath holy as our part of the bargain in our ancient Covenant with God -- and one of the most joyous and meaningful parts of the bargain at that.

In our Bible and in our tradition built upon the Bible, the Sabbath is a day of delight, a foretaste of redemption, of the World to Come. In order to find out how this is so, you have to empty your pockets!

Elliot B. Gertel
(adapted)

HOLY TIME 5

Four Besomim boxes. Late 19th century. Coll. Max Berger, Vienna, Austria. ©Photograph by Erich Lessing.

A PALACE IN TIME

The seventh day is the armistice in man's cruel struggle for existence, a truce in all conflicts, personal and social, peace between man and man, man and nature, peace within man; a day on which handling money is considered a desecration, on which man avows his independence of that which is the world's chief idol. The seventh day is the exodus from tension, the liberation of man from his own muddiness, the installation of man as a sovereign in the world of time.

In the tempestuous ocean of time and toil there are islands of stillness where man may enter a harbor and reclaim his dignity. The island is the seventh day, the Sabbath, a day of detachment from things, instruments and practical affairs as well as of attachment to the spirit.

...The Sabbath, thus, is more than an armistice, more than an interlude; it is a profound, conscious harmony of man and the world, a sympathy for all things and a participation in the spirit that unites what is below and what is above. All that is divine in the world is brought into union with God....

To set apart one day for freedom, a day on which we would not use the instruments which have been so easily turned into weapons of destruction, a day for being with ourselves, a day of detachment from the vulgar, of independence of external obligations, a day on which we stop worshipping the idols of technical civilization, a day on which we use no money, a day of armistice in the economic struggle with our fellow men and the forces of nature — is there any institution that holds out a greater hope for man's progress than the Sabbath?

Abraham Joshua Heschel
The Sabbath: Its Meaning For Modern Man

ROPING OFF TIME

Time. Jews have an amazing way with time. We create islands of time. Rope it off. Isolate it. Put it on another plane. In doing so, we create within that time a special aura around our everyday existence. Carving out special segments of holy time suits the human psyche perfectly, for ordinary human beings cannot live constantly at the peak of emotion. Thus, *Shabbat*, holy time, gives us an opportunity to experience that emotional peak, to feel something extraordinary in an otherwise ordinary span of time.

You would not think of time as having texture, yet, in a traditional Jewish household it becomes almost palpable. On *Shabbat*, I can almost feel the difference in the air I breathe, in the way the incandescent lamps give off light in my living room, in the way the children's skins glow, or the way the trees sway. Immediately after I light my candles, it is as if I flicked a switch that turned *Shabbat* on in the world, even though I know very well the world is not turned on to *Shabbat*. Remarkable as this experience is, even more remarkable is that it happens every seventh day of my life.

How does it happen? There will always be an element of mystery in transforming time from ordinary to extraordinary, but the human part of the process is not mysterious at all. It is not one great big leap or one awesome encounter with the Holy, but rather just so many small steps, like parts of a pattern pieced together.

Blu Greenberg
How To Run A Traditional Jewish Household

ONE WORD — AND TEARS

A number of years ago I was lecturing about a great religious personality named the Hofetz Haim, Rav Yisroel Meir Kagan. In the small town of Radin in Poland where he lived, there was a *yeshiva*, and a 16-year-old student was caught smoking on the Sabbath. The administration wanted to expel him. The Hofetz Haim asked permission to speak with the young man, after which he requested that the student remain in the *yeshiva*. He met with the young man for two minutes. The force of his personality was so great that the young man immediately became not only a dedicated student and a Sabbath observer, but ultimately a rabbi as well. As I was speaking, I noticed a gentleman sitting in the front row, an older man, who began trembling violently. He ran up to me at the end of the lecture. Rabbi," he said, "where did you hear that story?" I didn't remember. He moved me outside the hotel and said, "*Ani hagever*, it happened to me."

We walked around a little while, both of us silent. And I asked him, "What did the Hofetz Haim say to you? How did he influence you so profoundly?" He closed his eyes, almost looking into the past, and said: "One morning the Hofetz Haim stopped me, and he took my arm and invited me into his home. There wasn't one piece of furniture that was whole. There were maybe five or six books on the bookshelf. It was dire poverty. And this great rabbi took my hand and looked into my eyes, and he said just one word, he said 'Shabbos.' Then he began to weep, and his tears fell on the hand which was in his palm, my hand. If I live to 120, I'll never stop feeling the scalding heat of his tears. Then he said again that one word, 'Shabbos,' as if it contained the secret of the universe. He embraced me and led me gently outside."

Rabbi Shlomo Riskin
Hadassah Magazine

SABBATH PRAYER

God, help us now to make this new *Shabbat.*
After noise, we seek quiet;
After crowds of indifferent strangers,
We seek to touch those we love;
After concentration on work and responsibility,
We seek freedom to meditate, to listen to our inward selves.
We open our eyes to the hidden beauties
and the infinite possibilities in the world You are creating;
We break open the gates of the reservoirs
of goodness and kindness in ourselves and in others;
We reach toward one holy perfect moment of *Shabbat.*

Ruth Brin
Harvest: Collected Poems and Prayers

A DAY OF SPIRITUAL GROWTH

The civilization of a people is determined by how that people makes a living. The culture of a people is determined by how it lives. The degree of the civilization of a people may be measured by its achievements in the means *by which* man lives. Its culture may be measured by its achievements in the things *for which* man lives.

The material means which a person uses in his labors is the product of the civilization around him. The spirit in which he approaches his work, the purpose of his work, what he does with his material achievements — these are determined by his culture. Hence the close relationship between work and leisure, between man's creativity and the leisure which affords him the opportunity to think and to regenerate his creative will and the power to be re-creative.

The Jewish ideal of the Sabbath is, therefore, not an ideal of idleness but a day for spiritual and cultural re-creativity. It is not a negative day, a day of no work, but a day of spiritual growth. It is a day which is to give value and purpose to man's work on the other days. This relationship between work and leisure, between civilization and culture, is suggested in the commandment on the Sabbath: "Six days shalt thou work and rest on the seventh."

David Aronson
The Jewish Way of Life

FREEDOM AND THE SANCTIFICATION OF TIME

It is no coincidence that this commandment to sanctify time was given at the moment of freedom from Egypt. Slaves have no clear notion of time since it is not theirs to dispose of. Only free people, who have at least limited control over their time, can fill it with significant matters — and sanctify it. Thus, the concept of freedom and the sanctification of time are bound up with each other.

Ovadiah Sforno

EMBRACED BY THE *MITZVAH*

A Hasidic master once declared that the *mitzvah* of the *sukkah* is in one sense superior to all other *mitzvot*. "When I perform any other *mitzvah* the *mitzvah* is, as it were, outside me. But when I sit in the *sukkah* I have the *mitzvah* all around me and am embraced by it." Another Hasidic master declared that the Sabbath is superior even to the *sukkah*. "On *Sukkot* I am embraced by the *mitzvah* only when I am in the *sukkah*. But on the Sabbath I am embraced by the *mitzvah* wherever I am, wherever I go, and all through the day."

Louis Jacobs
The Book of Jewish Belief

THE SEED OF ETERNITY IS PLANTED IN THE SOUL

Six days a week we live under the tyranny of things of space; on the Sabbath we try to become attuned to holiness in time. It is a day on which we are called upon to share in what is eternal in time, to turn from the results of creation to the mystery of creation; from the world of creation to the creation of the world.

Six days a week we wrestle with the world, wringing profit from the earth; on the Sabbath we especially care for the seed of eternity planted in the soul. The world has our hands, but the soul belongs to Someone Else. Six days a week we seek to dominate the world; on the seventh day we try to dominate the self....

Abraham Joshua Heschel
The Sabbath

WHEN *SHABBAT* DOES THE GREATEST GOOD

Some people think that the Sabbath and the festivals can be kept when you are not too busy; but it is when you are busy and the pressure is at its maximum that the pause of the Sabbath will do you the greatest good.

Ben Zion Bokser

THE ETERNAL WITHIN THE TEMPORAL

The Sabbath has taught us how to sanctify time and bring a dimension of holiness into the profane rhythm of life; how to unite a way of thinking with a way of living and join body and soul, heart and mind to the service of God; how to be worthy of having been created in His image and touch the hem of the world-to-come in this world; how to find a foretaste of heaven on earth and sense the eternal within the temporal. If Israel had done nothing more than give the Sabbath to mankind, it would deserve to be called "the chosen people."

Samuel Dresner
The Sabbath

THERE IS NOTHING THAT CANNOT WAIT

Thus we testify and declare in the *Kiddush*: "And heaven and earth were finished and all there within them... and God finished on the seventh day His work which He had done and He rested from all the work which He had done.

Did He really finish all His work? Does He not continue to be involved in His creation every minute of the time? The sages of the Talmud find here a lesson for us to learn when we come to emulate God in the observance of His and our Sabbath. He finished all His work, they say, daringly. He acted *as if* He finished all His work. Likewise, one should feel and act on the Sabbath *as if* all one's work is done. The verse comes to teach us that even in this secular world of ours, it is possible to stop the world, get off for twenty-five hours, and feel as if everything is taken care of and done. There is nothing that cannot wait. God Himself showed us that it is possible. In the *kiddush* we testify to this fact.

Pinhas H. Peli
The Jewish Sabbath

SHABBAT-AGING

Sabot — S.A.B.O.T. were the crude wooden shoes worn by the French workers. Whenever the workers were abused by the factory owners more than usual, they would retaliate by throwing their sabots, their wooden shoes, into the machinery... sabotaging it. And thus we have the word "sabotage." Sabotage stopped the machinery. Thus I thought... Judaism also has a way of stopping the machinery. It's called *Shabbat*! We commit not "sabotage" but "*Shabbat*-age." Four thousand years ago our ancestors threw the *Shabbat* into the hum-drum evil and cease-less drudgery of the machinery of the world — "*Shabbat*-aging" it. And the world has never been the same.

Stanley Yedwab

SHABBAT WORKS

I know that you love your children. But when was the last time you took the time to tell them? *Shabbat* means holding your children — each child — blessing them and kissing them. *Shabbat* means that a week won't go by without our telling the people that we love the most that life wouldn't be what it is without them. *Shabbat* means that we won't accept invitations on Friday night to go out with another couple — *Shabbat* means regular, dependable time when children can count on their parents being home — when parents can count on their children being home.

Shabbat means that life is worth celebrating. Not once a year at a party — or not when we have to escape from it — on a vacation. Life — this life — with these people — is worth celebrating. Worth coming home Friday from a hard week of work and eating in the dining room — not the kitchen — with a table cloth and candles and wine — and a little bit more special dinner.

Worth going around the table and asking everyone to say something that happened in their week — because they are worth listening to.

We are all brought up to believe — adults and children — that what happens outside — in the world out there — is far more glamorous than anything inside.

But I know that it's not true. Ultimately the greatest richness is not out there — it's in here — in you — in your home. Give it time. At first, it's hard work.

I'll tell you something honestly. *Shabbat* works.

Shira Milgrom

SHABBOS HAS COME

A flare lights a sky of darkness,
Illuminating a moment.
Sparks of the soul make their way
into the everyday,
There is holiness in this hour.
These special moments bear hints of a
spiritual world, here and now.
That world beckons, entices,
Prodding us to respond with awe,
with a blessing, a prayer, an experience of the Holy.
To know the wonder of this hour.

Now, *Shabbos* has come. It is a day, all of delights.
A taste of the good world-to-come.
Every moment precious, a potential for good.
Not diverse sparks. A holy flame.
We feel the strength of the Sabbath's spiritual power
In prayer, in the Torah, in the synagogue, in the home.
In the candles and *kiddush*, in the clothes we wear,
and the words we speak.

May there be holiness in those words. May they be soft gentle words,
loving kindness and compassion
full of *chen*, full of *chesed*, full of *rachamim*.
May they help us to seek God's face, feel The Presence.
May every moment of this day be precious, dropping salvation
into our lives.
May there be holiness in this day.

Shabbos has come. We became partners with God in Creation.
We have grown. Now we rest.
A time of ends. Torah-talk of life and its purposes.
Of fish and fecundity. Of song and its lilt.
"This day is honored above all days; if I could declare for all:
Shabbat Hayom L'Adonoy. This Day Is For God."

Myron Fenster

REST IS FREEDOM

The Sabbath is the anticipation of the Messianic time, just as the Messianic period is called the time of "continuous Sabbath." In fact, the Sabbath is not only the symbolic anticipation of the Messianic time, but is considered its real precursor. As the Talmud puts it, "If all of Israel observed it fully only once, the Messiah would be here."

Resting, not working, then has a meaning different from the modern meaning of relaxation. In the state of rest, man anticipated the state of human freedom that will be fulfilled eventually. The relationship of man and nature and of man and man is one of harmony, of peace, of no interference. Work is a symbol of conflict and disharmony; rest is an expression of dignity, peace and freedom.

The Sabbath ritual has such a central place in the Biblical religion because it is more than a "Day of Rest" in the modern sense; it is a symbol of salvation and freedom. This is also the meaning of God's rest; this rest is not necessary for God because He is tired, but it expresses the idea that great as creation is, greater and crowning creation is peace; God's work is a condescension; He must "rest," not because He is tired but because He is free and fully God only when He has ceased work. So is man fully man only when he does not work, when he is at peace with nature and his fellow men; that is why the Sabbath commandment is at one time motivated by God's rest and at the other by the liberation from Egypt. Both mean the same and interpret each other; rest is freedom.

Erich Fromm
Forgotten Language

ON *SHABBAT* WE COME HOME

It is the Sabbath that can give the alienated individual a sense of home-coming. It was not so long ago, when Jewish artisans and peddlers, teachers and scribes, who during the week were working hard to eke out a living "on the road," would make every possible effort to be home "for *shabbes*." Yet coming home for the Sabbath always meant much more than physically returning home from work or business. It meant an "at-homeness" which would rarely be sensed during the week. The weekly Sabbath celebration brought on a family togetherness sparked with tenderness and intimacy impossible to achieve under the pressures of the weekly schedule. It gave parents the time and the relaxation to listen to their children, to talk to them, to smile at them; and it gave them time for one another.

Friday night, not unwittingly called in Hebrew *leil shabbat* ("Sabbath night") was never taken as a "free night" to "go out," as one can sleep late on the morning after. No. It was, and is, for Sabbath observers, a "night in." Very rarely does one leave home on Friday night, no matter what the occasion or whatever "function" is taking place outside. This custom must go back to Tannaitic times. The ancient Rabbis interpret the verse "And I shall give the rain of your land in its proper time" — when is the "proper time" for rain? On Friday night. Do you know why? Because everyone stays home on that night and rain is not going to trouble anyone.

As the Sabbath comes, we come home from our alienated existence in this strange world. We again encounter and honor the image of God in ourselves and in all human beings around us.

Pinhas H. Peli
The Jewish Sabbath

The perfect Sabbath rest is the attuning of the heart to the comprehension of God.

Maimonides
Tzavah, 101

The Holy One lends us an extra soul on the eve of the Sabbath, and withdraws it at the close of the Sabbath.

Simeon b. Lakish
Babylonian Talmud, Betza, 16a

HOW WE SANCTIFY TIME

The Sabbath itself is a spiritual sanctuary, a sanctuary in time. At the conclusion of the six days of creation, God blessed the seventh day and declared it holy.

By sanctifying the seventh day, God taught us that we too can sanctify time, we can add a dimension of holiness to every day.

We sanctify time when we believe in people, but we do not expect more from them than we are prepared to give.

We sanctify time when we welcome pleasure, but we realize that we miss the true meaning of life if pleasure is all we pursue.

We sanctify time when we strive to acquire new ideas but we also strive to surrender old prejudices.

We sanctify time when we work for material success, but we also treasure the things that money cannot buy.

We sanctify time when we seek companionship, but do not surrender our appreciation of solitude.

We sanctify time when we crave happiness, but we understand that the harvest of happiness is usually reaped by the hands of helpfulness.

We sanctify time when we yearn to be loved, but we also strive to make ourselves lovable.

We sanctify time when we pray as if everything depended on God, but we act as if everything depended on us.

Sidney Greenberg
Minhat Shabbat

PRAYER OF A JEWISH WOMAN
BEFORE LIGHTING *SHABBES* CANDLES

O God of Your people Israel:
You are holy
And You have made the Sabbath and the people of Israel holy.
You have called upon us to honor the Sabbath with light.
With joy
And with peace —
As a king and queen give love to one another;
As a bride and her bridegroom —
So have we kindled these two lights for love of your daughter,
The Sabbath day.

Translated from the Yiddish by Arthur Green
in *The Jewish Catalog*
by Michael Strassfeld and Richard Seigel

The Sabbath is the hub of the Jew's universe; to protect it is a virtue; to love it is a liberal education.

Israel Zangwill

SYMBOL AND INSTRUMENT OF SALVATION

But the Sabbath is not only a symbol of the salvation to be achieved by communion with God. It is itself an instrument that we may employ to advantage in our pursuit of salvation. We need perhaps more than ever before to terminate each week with a day that shall stimulate our thirst for salvation and keep us faithful to the ideals that lead to its attainment. Otherwise our mere pre-occupation with the business of "making a living," that is, of securing the conditions indispensable to life, tends to absorb all our attention, and life itself becomes empty and meaningless. We work to keep alive that we may work to keep alive, until our powers are spent in this weary treadmill, and death brings surcease of labor. If life is to be lived zestfully, and to employ all those human faculties the full exercise of which calls forth true joy in being alive, we dare not permit life to sink to such a level of mere preoccupation with the problem of survival. The Sabbath, with its insistence upon interrupting the routine of our daily business and concerning ourselves with spiritual values, helps to save us from such a fate.

Mordecai M. Kaplan (adapted)
The Meaning of God in Modern Jewish Religion

INVESTING TIME WITH SPECIAL MEANING

The sanctification of time is part of the Jewish pattern of investing life with holiness. In terms of real time, there is no difference between one hour and another. Differences appear when we impose "personal time" upon the undifferentiated hours. Thus, perhaps, some special occasions in our lives whose duration may be only a few moments may hold a place in our memory greater than many months or years.

The Sabbath and the Holy Days represent an attempt to take a block of time and invest it with special meaning. The idea behind it is to compel us to recognize the extraordinary in the ordinary, thus giving significance to both dimensions of life by setting aside a day for a break in the routine of daily living. By surrounding it with regulations designed to emphasize its sacredness, we heighten our sensitivity to time and experience.

Mordecai Waxman

AN ARCHITECT OF TIME

Just as a gifted space planner can be given 3000 feet of open office space — and by adding divisions, structures and furniture, he can create more space than was there before, so Judaism does the same with time. Judaism is a brilliant architect of time — *the* architect of time — and *Shabbat* its major work of art.

Shabbat works to create more time — by adding divisions and structures — by setting it off from the rest of the week. *Shabbat* works. Only, honestly, with one condition. You have to stick to it. Like any great relationship, it doesn't work without commitment.

Shira Milgrom

TO STAY IN TOUCH WITH WHAT IS PERFECT

We all have moments when the perfection of the world is revealed to us. A walk on the beach. A spectacular sunset. Our lover's eyes. A sleeping child. Sometimes, these moments take us by surprise, like rainbows. Sometimes, we engineer them: we plan vacations in the mountains, or tiptoe into the baby's room.

Shabbat is the way Jews arrange their lives to stay in touch with what is perfect in the world on a regular basis. It is Judaism's essential insight, its backbone, its methodology.

Diamant and Cooper
Living A Jewish Life

A DAY FOR RENEWING OURSELVES

One recurring theme in the liturgy and law of the Sabbath is that it is a day different from the other days of the week. That is true not only in what we do and do not do on the Sabbath; it is true also in how we feel on that day. On *Shabbat* we set aside the concerns of the week. It is almost as if we enter into a different world. Abraham J. Heschel tried to describe that experience through a metaphor that has become famous. He called the Sabbath "a palace in time." A palace is distinguished from the land around it by a moat. The moat also serves to protect it from attack. In the same way, the Sabbath is a time that is set aside. The laws of the Sabbath, like the moat around the palace, serve to protect the Sabbath day from the demands of the week. As a result, the Sabbath is a time in which we get to stop the rush and pressures of our daily existence and take time off to think about ourselves as people and as Jews, to gain perspective on what we do during the week, and to renew ourselves in every way.

Elliot N. Dorff
Knowing God: Jewish Journeys to the Unknowable

A NEW GIFT

We Jews should become missionary about *Shabbat*. It is too good — and too important — an idea to keep just for ourselves at this point in history. But before we can offer *Shabbat* to the world, we have to reclaim it for ourselves. To most Jews, real celebration of *Shabbat* is at best a distant memory. Others limit their *Shabbat* to the lighting of candles or attendance at synagogue, but do not allow themselves the full gift of a relaxing *Shabbat* day. The pressures working against *Shabbat* have been overwhelming, and the complex network of laws makes the traditional *Shabbat* seem to many like a day of restriction and constraint rather than one of joy. *Shabbat itself is in need of renewal.* It needs to be presented again to the Jewish people as a new gift, something being offered to us just this day.

Arthur Green
Reconstructionist Magazine

ACTION AND REST

Sabbath is the Jewish answer to the profound question all religions face about the relationship between doing and being, between what Indian mystics call *sat* (perfect being) and *prana* (spirit and energy). All religions must cope with the apparent contradiction between a vision of reality as ultimately changeless and one that contains contrast, opposition and change. In the Bible the key terms are not "being" and "energy" but "creation" and "rest." Viewed in this light, the idea of Sabbath is not naive or primitive at all. It is a highly sophisticated philosophical notion. It postulates an ultimate force in the universe which is not just passive and changeless but which acts and is acted upon. Yet it affirms what most religions also say about the ultimate: it is eternal and perfect. Sabbath links God and world and human beings in a dialectic of action and rest, of purposeful doing and "just sitting." The seventh day is holy to Yahweh, and one keeps it holy not by doing things for God or even for one's fellow human beings. One keeps it holy by doing nothing.

I think Hui-neng, the legendary sixth Zen patriarch, whose teaching constantly returned to learning how to do nothing, would understand Sabbath. I can almost see him, magically transported in a nineteenth-century Hasidic *shtetl* or into an ancient Jewish village on the seventh day, smiling appreciatively: these barbarians certainly had an inkling of the truth one day of the week at least. But what would disturb Hui-neng is that after sundown on the Sabbath, the Jews do begin again to live as though work and effort and time are real, as though action does make a difference and salvation has not yet come in its fullness. Maybe Hui-neng would swat a few behinds with his fan, or pull a few ears. But his efforts would be useless, because his reality and the reality of Moses are not the same. The difference is that Hui-neng views the world either as total transience or total stillness, and for him there is no real difference between the two. The Hebrew vision sees both acting and being, doing and non-doing, as equally real and equally important. By observing the rhythmic return to Sabbath, human beings reflect the divine reality itself.

Harvey Cox
Turning East

A COMMUNITY EXPERIENCE

The Sabbath is a time when not only families get together; the Jewish community does too. The community comes together to worship, study, and discuss communal concerns. From the twelfth century to the twentieth, the community even acted as a court of last resort: members who felt that justice had not been done in their cases could interrupt the prayers and have the community sit as a court of the whole. As you might imagine, as time went on restrictions were imposed on this right to insure that it was not used frivolously, but the use of Sabbath services for judicial matters shows clearly the extent to which the Sabbath was and is an occasion for the community.

The community gets together on the Sabbath in another sense as well. The Sabbath is a time not only for official meetings of the community for the purposes of worship, study, and public announcements, but also for informal contacts among friends. People commonly invite guests for one of the three Sabbath meals (dinner on Friday evening, lunch on Saturday, and, *Se'udah Sh'lee-sheet*, "the third meal," late Saturday afternoon), and *Shabbat* is a time for seeing and talking with friends at other times of the day, too.

Elliot N. Dorff
Knowing God: Jewish Journeys to the Unknowable

THE MESSIAH MAY TRAVEL ON *SHABBAT*

A *Hasidic* master once said: "I know that Elijah cannot come on the Sabbath because he is not allowed to travel on the sacred day. Yet, as a rabbi, I give him a dispensation to travel, since if only he will come many lives will be saved; the coming of the Messiah will mean an end to war. I take full responsibility; the saving of life takes precedence over the Sabbath. So he can come and need not worry about any desecration of the Sabbath."

A SHORT *AMIDAH*

They say we're supposed to be in a palace.
So we bow and take certain steps
as the prescribed supplication
drops from our lips.
But what do we really know
of castles and kings?
My kitchen faucet constantly leaks
and the kids' faces
usually need cleaning.
If a door opened to a real palace,
I'd probably forget
and carry in a load of groceries.

No, the door we stand in front of
when the *Amidah* begins is silence.
And when we open it
and step through,
we arrive in our hearts.
Mine's not a fancy place,
no jewels, no throne,
certainly not fit for a king.
But in that small chamber,
for just a few moments on Sabbath,
God and I can roll up our sleeves,
put some *schnapps* out on the table,
sit down together, and finally talk.
That's palace enough for me.

Sid Lieberman
Ra'ayonot

TO SHARE WHAT IS ETERNAL IN TIME

Six days a week we humans use time. We value it as a means to an end. Time "well spent" for us is time that helps us acquire something.

Yet to have more does not mean to be more. Indeed, there is a realm of time where the goal is not to have, but to be, not to own, but to give, not to control, but to share, not to subdue, but to be in accord. Life goes wrong when the control of space, the acquisition of things, becomes our sole concern.

The seventh day rights our balance and restores our perspective. It is like a palace in time and a kingdom for all. It is not a date, but an atmosphere.

On the seventh day, we celebrate time rather than space. Six days we live under the tyranny of things of space; on the seventh day we try to become attuned to holiness in time.

It is a day on which we are called upon to share in what is eternal in time. To turn from the results of creation to the mystery of creation; from the world of creation to the creation of the world.

Adapted from Abraham Joshua Heschel
The Sabbath

LONGING FOR AN ETERNAL *SHABBAT*

In *The Golden Chain (Di Goldene Keit)* by Y.L. Peretz, the Hasidic Rebbe refused "to make *Havdalah*" on Saturday night, because he wanted an "uninterrupted *Shabbos* in the universe" (*"shabbos soll sein oif der velt"*). As against this, the sad feeling frequently seizes us that in our day man refuses to recite *Kiddush* on *Erev Shabbat* in order that the universe be eternally secular. We have not yet experienced an uninterrupted *Shabbat*, but we have certainly experienced a succession of week days which have withered our souls and emptied them of their vital substance.

Yitzchak Maor
Reconstructionist Magazine

GOD, I HAVE TIME

And so all people run after time, God.
They pass through life running, hurried, jostled,
overburdened, frantic, and they never get there.
They still haven't time.
In spite of all their efforts, they're still short of time.
Of a great deal of time.

God, You must have made a mistake in Your calculations.
The hours are too short, the days are too short, our
lives are too short.
You who are beyond time, God, You smile to see us
fighting it.
And You know what You are doing.
You make no mistakes in Your distributions of time
to people.
You give each one time to do what You want him to
do.
But we must not deface time, waste time, kill time,
For time is not only a gift that You give us
But a perishable gift,
A gift that does not keep.

God, I have time.
I have plenty of time.
All the time You gave me.
The years of my life,
The days of my years,
The hours of my days,
They are all mine,
Mine to fill quietly, calmly
But to fill completely to the brim.

Michael Quoist
Gates of Shabbat

THE PAUSES BETWEEN THE NOTES

A great pianist was once asked by an ardent admirer: "How do you handle the notes as well as you do?" The artist answered: "The notes I handle no better than many pianists, but the pauses between the notes — ah! That is where the art resides."

In great living, as in great music, the art may be in the pauses. Surely one of the enduring contributions which Judaism made to the art of living was the *Shabbat,* "the pause between the notes." And it is to the *Shabbat* that we must look if we are to restore to our lives the sense of serenity and sanctity which *Shabbat* offers in such joyous abundance.

Sidney Greenberg
Likrat Shabbat

WHAT OUR SICK SOCIETY NEEDS

Our sick society needs the quietness engendered in a day kept holy.

Our madly rushing, neurotic society needs the therapy of the silence and quietness that flows from a day kept holy, really holy. A day when our thoughts are of God, our actions are tempered by a desire to serve God and our families, a day that is so different from other days that it could make us different in our relationships to God and to our fellow men.

Rev. Dr. Ernest R. Palen

PREPARING FOR *SHABBAT*

The six days of the week control our lives not only with their preponderant number of hours, but also because we drive ourselves, each day, to be productive, busy, and involved with the world. Consider the power of *Shabbat*, however. Though it is only one day, it can balance the other six.

There are times when we are not receptive to it, either because our ravishing of the world is so pleasurable that we are loath to put it aside, or because our involvements are so intricate or urgent that we are loath to suspend them. But it comes, offering us the opportunity to rise above everyday whims and compulsions. We can "remember" it and "keep it holy" — or forget our role as celebrants on this day, remembering only that we have come to identify ourselves as teachers, students, butchers, and bakers. Sometimes, *Shabbat* is difficult to observe — even unbearable. To overcome the difficulties requires discipline and energy. But having made the effort, it is equally difficult to return to the week, often as unbearable.

No one can adequately describe what *Shabbat* is. Each person will respond to it in his own way. It is a time, not a space, and so it cannot be grasped, only apprehended, experientially and individually. I can make the introductions, but the relationship is up to you. A few things to keep in mind, though, before getting into *Shabbat*:

1. As the saying goes, "Once is not enough." The surprise of understanding the power of *Shabbat* will not come for several weeks. Give yourself a two-month trial. If, after this time, you are not thoroughly pleased with *Shabbat*, go back to doing what you were doing before. If you are like most people who have tried it, you won't go back.

2. Do not do it alone. Doing *Shabbat* alone is like opening a gift alone.

3. Intend to do it. Anticipate it during the course of the week, particularly on Friday.

Singers do not walk from the street onto the stage and begin to sing. Athletes do not walk onto the field and begin competition immediately. Similarly, we cannot drive through rush hour, run through the doorway, and say, "*Shabbat Shalom*." This is a radically different pace. It requires transition — physically and mentally.

Richard Siegel
Moment Magazine

SHABBAT CANDLES   *6*

IN THE FOREST

The Sabbath is rightly at home in reborn Israel. The Sabbath meant home even while Jews were (or still are) "en route," and away from home. Chaim Nahman Bialik, the great Hebrew poet, tells a beautiful story of how his family when cruelly deported from its home in a village in Tsarist Russia, found itself desolately and aimlessly wandering in a forest. Suddenly, his mother realized that it was Friday afternoon and as sunset was approaching, she immediately pulled out from somewhere two little candles, lit them, covered her face to recite the blessing over the Sabbath and all at once "we were back home again." Between the stars flickering above and the Sabbath candles flickering below, they no longer felt uprooted and ashamed. While probably realizing subconsciously that the Sabbath was bound inevitably to come to an end, they were, for the time being, in a peaceful, serene home.

Pinhas H. Peli
The Jewish Sabbath

TO LIGHT CANDLES

To light candles in all the worlds —
that is *Shabbat*.
To light *Shabbat* candles
is a soul-leap pregnant with potential
into a splendid sea, in it the mystery
of the fire of sunset.
Lighting the candles transforms
my room into a river of light,
my heart sets in an emerald waterfall.

Zelda
Israeli, Yiddish Poet

WHEN WE MAKE IT DIFFERENT

At the turn of the 19th century a young Jew was leaving his home in the old world to take up life in the United States. He went to his Rabbi and asked for a blessing and a word of advice. The Rabbi said: "I am not going to tell you to observe the whole Torah. I shall not even advise you to be a God-fearing Jew. I ask only one little thing. Every week, when the Sabbath comes, put on a different garment." The young man asked, in surprise, "Is this all you ask?" "Yes," said the Rabbi, if you will remember that the Sabbath is different, you will have retained a great principle."

Sabbath observance is not as hard as it seems to those who stand on the outside. We can begin with a minimum program. First, we should beautify our homes spiritually. We know so much about interior decoration. We employ the best decorators to achieve proper color schemes and furniture arrangements. We have a bit of Jewish advice to offer. There is one simple object for our homes that will add more spiritual beauty than any expensive item that our interior decorators can provide.

Let us begin with a set of candlesticks. Let us light the candles on Friday night. Let there be the presence of the light, accompanied by the beautiful prayer that designates those candles as special — *Shabbat* candles. They will sanctify our homes, and speak to our children in a silent language that is unforgettable. The burning candles will proclaim: This is a Holy Day! Tonight we dedicate our thoughts to all that is joyous and spiritual in life.

The second suggestion we would make is that we set a Sabbath table. We are not speaking of an expensive table setting. We mean a table that at least one night a week is a family table. The keynote is a togetherness which the entire family shares, a unity that binds all family members together in love and in loyalty. I know of no restaurant that can reproduce the spirit of sanctity that the humblest *Shabbat* table possesses when the family is gathered around it; when they break *Hallah* together and drink the wine of the *Kiddush* over which the blessing has been chanted.

Ralph Simon

SHABBAT IN THE GULAG

Yosef Mendelovitch, a former Soviet refusenik now lives in Israel. Before his release, he was imprisoned in a Soviet gulag. He recalls how he managed to observe the *Shabbat*:

In preparation for the Sabbath, I washed the cell's floor with water. The cell is made of cement. Each prisoner has a rag, which I wet with water from the faucet. Even this act of floor-washing gave me the distinct feeling that, despite the poor condition, I had done something to prepare for the Sabbath.

I would don a clean white shirt, sent to me by my father during the first year of my imprisonment. Of course, it was strictly forbidden to have any civilian clothing, but I was able to keep it on the pretext it was an undershirt. I would wear it every Sabbath, symbolizing something new and white. After the conclusion of the Sabbath, I would wash it out as carefully as possible, putting it aside to be used again on the next Sabbath.

I also kept with me a clean handkerchief which I used as a *challah* cover. During the whole week, I would divide my bread rations up in such a way as to be able to have enough available to observe the Sabbath. By the Sabbath, I'd have two pounds of bread. Then I could at least eat to satisfy the appetite I'd been building up all week.

I'd repeat the same procedure with the fish we received, since on the Sabbath it's the custom to eat fish. The fish could be set aside, for it's salted and thus easily preserved. It was somewhat dangerous to set aside food, for if it was discovered during a search there would be hard questions asked. The guards have two suspicions: first, that you're setting aside food for a prison break, and second, that perhaps one of the guards is bringing you extra food, contrary to regulations.

Yosef Mendelovitch
The Jewish Week

HOW ARE THE CANDLES LIT?

Usually when you perform a *mitzvah* requiring a blessing, you recite the blessing, and then perform the act. For example, with the *Kiddush*, the blessing is recited first and then the wine is drunk. However, kindling the *Shabbat* candles follows a different procedure. Since the blessing marks the formal beginning of *Shabbat*, and since according to the traditional definition of work lighting a fire on *Shabbat* is prohibited, you first light the candles (technically before *Shabbat*) and then recite the blessing (thereby beginning *Shabbat*).

In many homes it is customary for those who light the candles to cover their eyes or use their hands to block the candles from view while saying the blessing. Custom has it that at this moment, when the candles are not seen, it is as if the candles had not been lit. When the blessing is complete and *Shabbat* has begun, the candles are then revealed as lit.

Gates of Shabbat

IN A NAZI TRANSPORT

The train dragged on with its human freight. Pressed together like cattle in crowded trucks, the unfortunate occupants were unable even to move. The atmosphere was stifling. As the Friday afternoon wore on, the Jews and Jewesses in the Nazi transport sank deeper and deeper into their misery.

Suddenly an old Jewish woman managed with great effort to move and open her bundle. Laboriously, she drew out two candlesticks and *halla*. She had just prepared the *halla* for *Shabbat* when she was dragged from her home that morning. They were the only things she had thought worth taking. Soon the *Shabbat* candles lit up the faces of the tortured Jews and the singing of *Leha Dodi* transformed the scene. *Shabbat*, with its atmosphere of peace had descended upon them all.

Likrat Shabbat

THE SABBATH CANDLES TRANSFORMED US

There was another element of that life that I loved. Friday night. It was a time when, by the magic of the Sabbath candles, we were transformed into a happy, picture-book family. The recriminations and bickering would cease and the music would begin. Dov was just a baby at the time, but Shalom and I would sit at the gleaming white table in our "*Shabbat* outfits," dark blue pants and white cotton shirts open at the collar.

When, a little while later, my father returned from the synagogue, we lined up in front of him for the Sabbath blessing, our eldest, Shalom, first and then me. "May God make you like Ephraim and Menashe," he said invoking the two grandsons of Jacob who, as Joseph's children, were especially beloved. Bending down to reach us, my father cradled our heads between his strong hands as he recited the blessing. "May He bless you and keep you... and give you peace."

My father, who worked hard all week managing and selling real estate, became our rabbi and cantor on Friday night. He took us through the meal singing the joyous melodies of the *Hasidim* and the resolute songs of the *Chalutzim*, the Israeli pioneers who, we were told, were singing the same songs as they worked to turn the desert green. My mother, a confirmed "listener" rather than singer, hummed along with a smile of contentment on her face.

Ari L. Goldman
The Search For God At Harvard

Shabbat Memories   7

SHABBAT CONFERRED AN AURA OF LOVE

I shall never forget *Shabbat* in my town. When I shall have forgotten everything else, my memory will still retain the atmosphere of holiday, of serenity pervading even the poorest houses; the white tablecloth, the candles, the meticulously combed little girls, the men on their way to the synagogue. When my town shall fade into the abyss of time, I will continue to remember the light and the warmth it radiated on *Shabbat*. The exalting prayers, the wordless songs of the *Hasidim*, the fire and radiance of their Masters....

The jealousies and grudges, the petty rancors between neighbors could wait. As could the debts and worries, the dangers. Everything could wait. As it enveloped the universe, the *Shabbat* conferred on it a dimension of peace, an aura of love.

Elie Wiesel
A Jew Today

THE *SHABBAT* I'LL NEVER FORGET

"Shabbat in Warsaw. The large group of us walking to *shul* while singing and dancing was like the actual March all over again. Services in the synagogue were incredible when you realized that it hadn't been that full for years. I could also practically feel the presence of the people who had prayed there years ago. I felt like we were breathing new life into it. Even more incredible was our walk from *shul* back to the hotel. Once again, we were dancing and singing songs. Most Polish people in the streets just stopped and stared at us with blank stares. But, there were a few Polish people who began to clap along with us and smile. It made me feel so incredible. I'll never forget it."

Deborah Chasan of Philadelphia
Participant in the 1992 March of the Living

IN THE *SHTETL*

You must make up your mind that Tevyeh the coolie, or Tevyeh the
dairyman, simply will not work ... from sundown on Friday to sundown on Saturday. No labour-leader in the world has ever been so
insistent on the forty-eight or forty-hour week as Tevyeh on his six-day
week. The Sabbath is the Lord's day; that is, it is Tevyeh's day for rest
in the Lord. He will not work on that day, he will not carry money
about, he will not touch fire or tear paper or do anything that savours
of the slavery of the body.... You will neither bribe, bully, nor per-
suade him into such transgress. For the Sabbath and the festivals are
all that are left to him; they are the last citadel of his freedom. On
those days he will pray, meditate, and refresh his spirit with a little
learning. He may be hungry; he will contrive to rise above it. He may
not know where the next day's food will come from, either; he will
contrive to forget that, too....

There never was such obstinacy! It must not be thought, either, that
Tevyeh, crushed under the double burden of the Jewish exile and the
worker's slavery, clings to these practices merely as a grim protest.
Not by any means. He enjoys them, thoroughly. He loves the Sabbath
and the festivals. He loves prayer.

And meanwhile the Sabbath is slipping away, the Queen is preparing
her departure, the harsh world, the daily struggle, the bitterness of life,
stand at the gates of the evening. Get everything you can out of this
heavenly interlude, an hour or two of prayer, an hour or two of study,
in the synagogue or at home. Till the moment of the Separation comes,
and with incense box uplifted, his family gathered about him, the
Kasrilevkite takes regretful leave of the Sabbath, and his wife sings, in
homely Yiddish, the valedictory of Reb Isaac of Berditchev, Reb Levi
Isaac the Compassionate....

What kind of Sabbath is it, I ask you, which leaves the world around
you utterly unchanged from the week-days? The shops are open, the
market-place is filled, the horses neigh, buyers and seller chaffer, the
[streetcar] thunders past the synagogue, and the Sabbath siesta is a
day-mare in a din of blaring radios and yelling children playing base-
ball in the street. And... traditionalists and modernists alike remember
now and again with a nostalgic pang the far-off magic of those sacred
hours, those transfigured interludes of the Sabbaths and festivals for
which even progress and freedom have found no substitute.

Maurice Samuel
The World of Sholom Aleichem

MY MOTHER-IN-LAW'S
ONE WAY CONVERSATION WITH GOD

Even better than *shul* is my mother-in-law's Friday-night *davening*. Occasionally, she spends a *Shabbat* with us. As I lurk around a corner, and listen intently, I feel as if I am privy to a private audience with God. She finishes up the regular Friday-night prayers, and then, in a barely audible whisper, and looking into her *siddur* all the while, she proceeds to carry on a one-way conversation with Him.

With eighty-five years behind her, my mother-in-law brings God up-to-date on the whereabouts and doings of each child, grandchild, and great-grandchild, occasionally summing up past favors and events of yesteryear. Once, more than fifteen years after I had been married, she reminded God that her son had married a nice *yiddishe maidele* (Jewish girl). After describing what each of us was doing, she turned His attention to the grandchildren — which school each attended, who was graduating, who was in a cast with a torn cartilage, and who was going to camp for a month. Rarely does she make an outright plea, but once she mentioned in passing that my brother-in-law's blood pressure was too high. Yet another time, she informed her beloved God that her grandson, then twenty-eight, chief resident at Peter Bent Brigham Hospital in Boston, was working very hard and had no time yet to look for a wife (hint, hint). Systematically, every Friday night she parades the entire family before God. Without ever using those words, it is a prayer of thanksgiving. May I be forgiven for eavesdropping, hers are truly among the most moving prayers I have ever heard.

Blu Greenberg
How to Run a Traditional Jewish Household

Happy is he whose mother has stroked his head on the Sabbath eve.
S. J. Agnon

ON NEW YORK'S LOWER EAST SIDE

The Irish and Italian boys had Christmas once a year; we had exaltation every Friday. In the most populous neighborhood of the world, rent by the shouts of peddlers, the screams of children, and the myriad noises of the city, there was every Friday evening a wondrous stillness, an eloquent silence. So quiet was it that two blocks from the synagogue you could hear the muffled chant of the cantor and the murmured prayers of the congregation. Once the service was over, you came home to find your mother dressed in her wedding dress with a white silk scarf around her head. And your father told you all the sufferings throughout the centuries were dedicated for this moment, the celebration of the Sabbath.

Harry Golden
The Greatest Jewish City in the World

WHY ZAIDA CRIED

We kids would gather in a dark room, like this, while Zaida, our grandfather, would light the *Havdalah* candle. Zaida couldn't stand to say *Havdalah* right away; he wanted *Shabbos* to stay as long as possible, so we would stand in the dark while he talked to us. He liked to say, "You know why this candle melts? Because it's more than a candle; it's the heart of *Shabbos*. You see, just like we don't want to leave it, it doesn't want to leave us. So it cries and melts tears. I don't want to go, it says, I've been your queen, your bride for one whole glorious day. If only I could stay with you the other six days." And then Zaida would say very sadly, "If only she could; if only we had her the other six days of the week. If only her happiness and peace could live in people's hearts the whole week long."

Once, after hearing this, I looked up at Zaida and said, "Don't cry, Zaida, see the melted tears? They're all over your hands. If you don't wash the wax off your fingers, *Shabbos* will be with you all week long. You can have *Shabbos* with you every single day, if you just decide to."

Zaida smiled at me and sighed, "If only we could decide not to wash the wax off our fingers... if only we could decide that."

Philip Arian
He Kindled a Light: A Philosophy of Jewish Education

SHABBAT IS...

my father's hands on my head as he whispers
"*Yevarech'cha*";
my mother's hands caressing the candleglow;
the taste for wine, the shine of silver, the scent of roses;
my wife's secret smile as she walks upstairs;
walking to synagogue, in sunshine, rain or snow;
my old rabbi's tales of wisdom and wonders;
the cantor's arabesque of faraway beauty;
turning to greet the Queen, the Bride;
soft night dreams and sweet daydreams;
a special color of the sky, a sacred rustle of the trees;
solace, healing, peace, laughter, song and stillness;
holy pages slowly turned, the kiss of ancient truths;
meeting anew my God, my people, my soul;
the fusion of long past days, of a good future, of a
timeless Now;
three stars aflame on a darkening sky;
the smell of cloves, the many-hued glory of the pleated
candle;
joy, safety, fullness, life.

Shabbat Is...
my hands on my grandchild's head as I whisper
"*Yevarech'cha*."   Andre Ungar

THE ADDITIONAL SOUL

The Jews of Lithuania were not in the habit of pampering themselves but when the Sabbath arrived the body assumed an importance to which it could never have aspired during the six working days of the week. It would begin on the Sabbath Eve. Ordinary Jews in those parts did not go to the ritual bath to cleanse themselves in honor of the Sabbath; they simply went to the bathhouse where, along with the workday sweat, they washed from their bodies the weekday world itself. Once it left the bathhouse thoroughly cleansed and made worthy of the Sabbath, the body was fit to taste some of the Sabbath's delights. And when the Sabbath Queen herself arrived, she poured forth her blessings beyond all measure upon the Jew — blessings over each man's table, to each according to his station, the blessing of rest for everyone alike, and the more the body needed them, the more it could relish the delights of sweet repose.

In brief, the Sabbath treated the body as true nobility. Still, her principal guest was not the body, but that which dwelt within it. It was with the soul that the Sabbath communed through the candle lights, through the melody welcoming the Angels of Peace, though the chant of the *Kiddush* and even through the food, flavored with the rare and singular spice called the Sabbath. The Sabbath spoke, too, in the recital of the Song of Songs, and in the study of the weekly Scriptural reading, twice in the original and once in the ancient Aramaic translation. The Sabbath conversed long with the soul that dwells in the secret places, a conversation which cannot be retold but which we know was a sacred dialogue. Could this soul with which the Sabbath communed so intimately be the same as that which had dwelt within man on the day before, or on Thursday, or on Wednesday.

It was indeed the same soul, but with a difference, for now it was enriched the *neshama yetera,* the "additional" soul. A poetic exaggeration? No, it was the name of something very real which every Jew could sense on his Sabbath day, and which no one can ever perceive or comprehend who has not tasted the flavor, the fragrance of the genuine Jewish Sabbath.

Avraham Kariv
Lithuania Land Of My Birth

The World Belongs To Our Creator

8

THE SABBATH SPEAKS TO THE HUMAN SOUL

The highest contribution of the Sabbath is in what it speaks to the human soul. It is a reminder of God as Creator of the universe. We know that creation in its fullest unfolding involved a time proven longer than a week as counted by a mortal's sense of time. The Biblical story of creation aims, however, in another direction. It divides time, as man reckons it, into two stages. One is the time of *becoming*, when things are made, when the world submits to the creative shaping of the divine order imposing itself on it; it is the time when we face the zone of the unfinished, the imperfect, waiting for the next step in the conquest of chaos by harmony, in the banishment of darkness by light breaking in on it. The second stage of time is the zone where God's glory shines with the splendor of His design in fulfillment. And each week is divided into these two time zones, the one to remind us of the work that needs to be done, the other, the Sabbath, to contemplate God's perfection which is discernible in all things He has made. The Sabbath celebrates God's work as Creator. It opens our hearts to the vision of the world as the theater of God's creative endeavors. And it sensitizes us to the knowledge of our own privilege as participants in the stupendous drama of God's creative work unfolding itself in the world.

Ben Zion Bokser
Judaism: Profile of a Faith

THE WORLD IS NOT OURS

Abstinence from work is the sign by which we are to demonstrate that God is the creator of heaven and earth, that He is also our Creator and that we too belong to Him, that all powers are His, and are consecrated to His service.

For six days the world belongs to us, for six days we may exercise our dominion over everything that our God has created, and perform *m'lachah*; we may stamp our creative impress on everything and make it the agent of our will, the executor of our purpose. But on the seventh day we shall testify that, after all, the world is not ours, that we are not its lord and master, but merely God's vassal on earth, that we only live and work by God's grace, that He is our Lord and Master, the Lord and Master of the smallest as of the greatest creature within our ken. To this we shall testify by giving the world its freedom on this day, by retiring into that sphere which is subject to ourselves... The bird, the fish, the animal that we refrain from tearing up, the material that we refrain from fashioning or chiselling, cutting or mixing, moulding or preparing, all this inaction is but a demonstration of homage to God, proclaiming Him Creator and Master and Lord of the world.

Samson Raphael Hirsch

The Sabbath has been instituted as an opportunity for fellowship with God, and for glad, not austere, service of God.

Judah Halevi
Kuzari, c. 1135, 3.5

AN ESSENTIAL AFFIRMATION OF FAITH

The Sabbath signifies an abdication on that day of the right to be master of certain things enjoyed during the six other days. It means not only resting oneself, but letting all other things rest: creating nothing — neither fire nor sound, excepting when it be for the sake of the Creator Himself. A Sabbath so observed... is an essential affirmation of faith.

Israel Meir Kagan

THE WEEKLY REMINDER

The *Mitzvot* are divine commands for me both because they have come to be such through the long history of my people and because they speak to my situation as a human being in need of God.

I keep the Sabbath, irrespective of its origins, because it is the fundamental religious institution of my people, as a people dedicated to God's service; because of the wealth of meaning the prophets and poets, the saints and sages of Israel have read into it; and because my personal religious life is enriched immeasurably by the weekly reminder that God is my Maker and Creator of all.

Louis Jacobs
as adapted in Likrat Shabbat

"REMEMBER" AND "OBSERVE"

The Rabbis note that the Fourth Commandment in Exodus 20, starts with the words "Remember the Sabbath," and in Deuteronomy 5, the same Fourth Commandment begins with the words "Observe the Sabbath." They make an interesting comment on this variation. They say that when it is not possible to observe the Sabbath, one can at least remember it; that when we cannot observe a "*mitzvah*," we can at least try to remember it.

This commandment to "remember a *mitzvah*," even when we cannot observe it, is one that we should always bear in mind. We often find ourselves in situations when we cannot observe all the laws of the Sabbath. But there is always something that we can do to remind ourselves that it is the Sabbath Day, and to recall the two main teachings of the Sabbath: the equality of all people before God, and our duty to live in accordance with those powers within us which make us God-like. If we try, at least, to remember when we cannot observe, then when the opportunity will present itself for us to observe, we will be more anxious and ready to do so.

Irwin Groner

To observe the Sabbath is to bear witness to the Creator.

Mekhilta, to Exodus 20.13

GIVING UP CONTROL

On the Sabbath, Jews celebrate God as the Creator. They abstain from many activities in recognition that they and the world result from the act of creation. Awe, wonder, and humility are expressed by giving up mastery and control over the world for a day. Nature is not our absolute possession. We are allowed and indeed commanded, however, to resume control temporarily as soon as human life itself is threatened. The Sabbath, therefore, does not force us to choose between a theocentric focus on the world and the dignity and significance of human existence. The vitality of the covenantal spirit demands that one maintain both poles with extreme seriousness. A religious humanism that ignores the religious vitality and power of awe and reverence before the infinite power and mystery of divinity violates the theocentric pole of Judaism. At the other extreme, a yearning to get beyond finitude and inhabit eternity is a violation of the dignity of human freedom and responsibility found in the covenantal concern for history.

David Hartman
A Living Covenant

NOT MASTERS

Man was created to harness and exploit the forces of nature — to "subdue the earth and have dominion over... every living thing...." (Gen. 1:28). To exercise such mastery over the universe and its immense forces is man's privilege. But only within limits. In two areas — one, of place and the other, of time — the Jew must renounce the assertion of his mastery over nature and return it to God, to be reminded that there is a Master above him after all. By proscribing for the Jew the operation of machines on the Sabbath — the sanctuary of time— and in the synagogue — the sanctuary of space, Judaism seeks to secure one impregnable refuge from the tyranny of automation....

On the Sabbath we are to be creatures, not creators; for once we are to be servants, not masters, so that we shall remember always to subordinate the scientific urge for mastery to the religious urge for service. Thus the Sabbath and the synagogue are to remind us that the highest achievement of the human intellect lies less in our ability to create than in our knowledge of how to control our creations and preserve our supremacy over them. On such knowledge, as we now realize, the survival of mankind will ultimately depend.

Immanuel Jakobovitz
"Jewish Law Faces Modern Problems"

HIGHER THAN SUCCESS

There are objectives in life which are higher than success. The Sabbath, with its exhortation to the worship of God and the doing of kind deeds, reminds us, each week, of these higher objectives. It prevents us from reducing our life to the level of a machine.

The Sabbath is one of the glories of our humanity. For if to labor is noble, then to pause, willingly, in that labor which may lead to success, money, or fame, may be nobler still.

To dedicate one day a week to rest and to God, is a prerogative and privilege unique to human beings. It is an ordinance which we may rightly call Divine.

C.G. Montefiore
as adapted in *Likrat Shabbat*

SAVED FROM SELF-IDOLIZATION

If prophets such as Isaiah and later on the Rabbis could look upon the observance of the Sabbath as the central axis of all of Judaism, it was because they saw in it the crystallization of the most basic Jewish tenets regarding our relationship to nature and God. Viewed from this vantage point, the prohibition against "purposeful activity" emerges as a much-needed reminder to us that we, too, are merely creatures of God. We must beware lest we become intoxicated with our success in conquering nature and fall victim to arrogant self-idolization. To be sure, human creativity and mastery over nature represent perfectly legitimate activities. We Jews have never shared the stance of the Promethean myth which condemns human creativity as an act of defiance against heavenly powers. But with all our endorsement of human creativity which has produced the miracles of civilization, we recognize the debilitating spiritual hazards that loom in the wake of our triumphs over nature. We are apt to forget that the universe — including our own capacity for creativity — is not a self-contained unit, but belongs to the Creator. Because of the regularity and order prevailing within the realm of nature, we are prone — especially in the "secular city" — to overlook the divine source of all existence. Thus the Sabbath saves us from the idolatry of science and technology. It reveals what nature conceals: the world is not a self-sufficient cosmos, but the continuous creation of God.

This theme is stressed in Exodus where it is affirmed that "the seventh day is the Sabbath unto God and thou shalt not perform any kind of work." No mention is made here of rest, relaxation, or other human benefits. The emphasis here is unmistakably theocentric. Humanity, as it were, is put in its place. The Sabbath makes us realize that we have a legitimate right to harness the forces of nature for creative work only if we refrain from self-deification and look upon ourselves as creatures charged by our Creator with the task of imitating Him by completing the task of creation.

Pinhas H. Peli
The Jewish Sabbath

I AM NOT AN ABSOLUTE MASTER

In observing the Sabbath, I became fully conscious that God alone is the Creator of the universe. The Sabbath, awakening my sense of creatureliness, directs me to understand that I must not relate to nature and to other persons as an absolute master. And so, in observing the Sabbath, I am educated to realize that all those who work for me must never be reduced to instruments serving my needs.

David Hartman
A Living Covenant

THE REAL PURPOSE OF LIFE

"...the real purpose of life is not to conquer nature but to conquer the self; not to fashion a city out of a forest but to fashion a soul out of a human being; not to build bridges but to build human kindness; not to learn to fly like a bird or swim like a fish but to walk on the earth like a man; not to erect skyscrapers but to establish mercy and justice; not to manufacture an ingenious technical civilization but to be holy in the midst of unholiness. The real tasks are to learn how to remain civilized in the midst of insanity; how to retain a share in man's dignity in the midst of the Dachaus and Buchenwalds, how to keep the mark of Cain from obscuring the image of the divine, how to fashion a home of love and peace, how to create children obedient and reverent, how to find the strength to perform the *mitzvot*, how to bend our will to God's will."

Samuel Dresner
The Sabbath

SHABBAT — THE BRIDE

"On the seventh day God ended His work of creation."

What can this possibly mean?
Is the seventh day a day of work?

It is like the case of a king who
made for himself a bridal canopy.

He painted it and panelled it.

What was still lacking
when the work was done?

A bride to enter it.

In the same way,
what was the world still lacking
when God had completed the work
of creation?

A bride to enter it.

So God brought His work to an end
not *on* the seventh day, but *with*
the seventh day: the bride, *Shabbat.*

Bereshit Rabbah 10

THE SEVENTH COIN

The Chinese relate a very striking parable. They say: "It came to pass that a man went to market, having on his shoulder a string of seven large copper coins. (Chinese coins are strung on strings and carried on the shoulders.) Meeting a beggar who was pleading for alms, the man gave the beggar six of his seven coins. Then the beggar, instead of showing gratitude, slipped up behind the man and stole the seventh coin.

"That is a strange parable," you say, but not so. Are there not many people who accept from God the gift of six days to do their labor and then, instead of being grateful, they steal from Him the seventh — the Sabbath — also?

Anonymous

A Day Of Harmony Rest And Peace

9

I NEED MORE TIME

What do I want to take home from my summer vacation? I close my eyes and think. Time. That is what I would like. The wonderful luxury of being at rest. The days when you shut down the mental machinery that keeps life on track and let life simply wander. The days when you stop planning, analyzing, thinking and just are.

I don't know why it is so hard to find the same piece of time during the rest of the year. Life is more frenzied, I am told by friends. They say this philosophically, as if "it" were in charge and we had lost control.

The people I know live within the confines of their weeks-at-a-glance. When more is demanded of us, we get larger datebooks with more elaborate planners. We fit things in.

We schedule — family, work, friendships. We organize with a fury of split-second timing. But we almost never pencil in time to do nothing.

It gets harder every year to figure out what separates our own lives from those of the creature frantically working the goldenrod beside me against a deadline of frost. What is the difference? A soul, the theologians say, a sense of mortality, a sabbath. Maybe it is the last, a day of rest, that we have lost first.

Ellen Goodman
Philadelphia Inquirer

A TIME TO LOOK AT THE SKY

Looking out the window on a weekday morning, the Chasidic teacher, Nachman of Bratzlav, noticed his disciple, Chaim, rushing along the street.

Reb Nachman opened the window and invited Chaim to come inside. Chaim entered the home and Nachman said to him, "Chaim, have you seen the sky this morning?" "No, Rebbe," answered Chaim. "Have you seen the street this morning?" "Yes, Rebbe." "Tell me, please, Chaim, what did you see in the street?" "I saw people, carts, and merchandise. I saw merchants and peasants all coming and going, selling and buying."

"Chaim," said Nachman, "in 50 years, in 100 years, on that very street there will be a market. Other vehicles will then bring merchants and merchandise to the street. But I won't be here then and neither will you. So, I ask you, Chaim, *what's the good of your rushing if you don't even have time to look at the sky?*"

Gates of Shabbat

ALL WOUND UP

My vote for the cleverest ad of the year is the one that was done by
some advertising agency for a hotel chain. Remember it? A picture of
a business executive with a Brooks Brothers suit and an attache case
rushing to his next appointment and coming out of his back is a large
key, the kind that is used to wind up mechanical toys — and the
advertisement below the picture said: if you are all keyed up, unwind
at our hotel.

We all remember that ad and we all identified with it for we are all
keyed up, tense people. We all live rushed, hectic, pressured lives.
We all feel harassed and driven and so we all responded to that ad.
We all had a sense of: hey, he's talking about me — when we saw it,
for we are all wound up.

The greatest killers in our society are not heart disease or cancer or car
accidents. The greatest killers are the clock, the calendar, and the
telephone. These are the things that strain and shorten our lives.

A Swiss psychiatrist by the name of Dr. Alex Farber recently came up
with a great idea. He has opened up a series of fancy resorts that he
calls SANE ASYLUMS, places that sane people can go to when they
feel themselves going under, when they feel that the pressure is becoming too great, places that you can go to prevent a breakdown. He
has one in Vienna, one in Brazil, one in Japan, and one in Acapulco.
And the difference between his resorts and others is that at his there
are no schedules, no time tables, no activities. You can eat breakfast at
7:00 AM or at 8:00 AM or at 9:00 AM or not at all, and the same with the
rest of the day. And that idea has attracted a great many people for all
of us feel so caught up in schedules and deadlines and rat races. You
know that sign that you see on a great many desks: I am going to have
a nervous breakdown next week if I can work it into my schedule.
That's a joke, and it is also a half truth for we all feel that way.

May I suggest that we Jews have been running sane asylums for a
great many years before Dr. Farber, we just didn't have the name. We
call it *Shabbes*. A day for being with our families, a day for being in
Shule, a day for living like a *mentsch*, a day for living and a day for
loving, a day for study and prayer and song and food and drink, a day
for getting away from the office and the mail and the bills and the

meetings and the telephone, a day for human living. And if your fathers needed the Sabbath in previous centuries, when life was far less pressured than it is today, then surely we need it a million times more.

Jack Reimer

RENEWAL AND THE ART OF LIVING

An artist cannot be continually wielding a brush. An artist must stop painting at times to freshen his or her vision....

Living is also an art. We dare not become so absorbed in its technical processes that we lose our consciousness of its general plan....

The Sabbath represents those moments when we pause in our brush-work to renew our vision. Having done so, we take ourselves to our painting with clarified vision and renewed energy. This applies to the individual and to the community alike.

Mordecai M. Kaplan
The Meaning of God in Modern Jewish Religion

WE NEED REGENERATION

With recurrent insistence, every tired fiber of our being cries out: "Rest, rest!" What is our instinctive reaction? Away we go for a brief vacation and, upon our return, we discover that we are even more exhausted than when we "took a break from the job." What we now need is a vacation to recuperate from our vacation. Why? Because our inter- mezzo was merely physical and what we desperately need is some- thing far more essential: a mental change of pace and spiritual change of mood.

We must periodically liberate ourselves from the tiresome monotony of day-to-day routine so that we may establish a mood of peace and tranquility; not merely a physical withdrawal from mundane activity, but a reconciliation with ourselves, in harmony with our own inner being. We must periodically and consistently seek mental and spiritual regeneration, release and emancipation from the slavery of materialism and worldly cares. The Sabbath Day is consecrated to God, prayer, and study; to the beauty and holiness of life, to the companionship of family and friends. It enables us to break the shackles of routine and restore our eroded humanity.

Hillel Silverman
Judaism Looks At Life

THE PAUSE THAT REFRESHES

Every beat of your heart is followed by a pause.

The first action of the heart is called a systole, and this is followed by a period of relaxation known as a diastole. Because this second function is so vital to life, it is sometimes referred to in medical circles as "the pause that refreshes."

The Jewish tradition has likewise formulated a pattern of six days of work followed by a day of relaxation. That day of spiritual refresh- ment is known as *Shabbat*, the Sabbath, which literally means "rest- ing." Just as the heart cannot function well without regular rest, so a person cannot live properly without a regular day of relaxation and spiritual refreshment.

Bernard S. Raskas
Heart of Wisdom

THE SABBATH SETS US FREE

By calling us away from our work, the Sabbath reminds us that "being" is both deeper and higher than "doing," that sometimes we have to stop doing what we do in order to start being who we are. To pause, to take stock of our lives, to contemplate the way we have come and the way we are going, is not reserved for Yom Kippur alone; every Sabbath offers us an opportunity for self-assessment, a liberation from the structures that define us, so we may be free to define ourselves in the eternal light of the Infinite. On the Sabbath we are freed to stand before God and to "know before Whom we stand," from Whom we have come, to Whom we must give ultimate account of our lives.

Michael S. Kogan

This is the meaning of the Jewish Sabbath, to give to man peaceful hours, hours completely diverted from everyday life, seclusion from the world in the midst of the world.

Leo Baeck
Essence of Judaism

WHY WE NAP ON *SHABBAT*

One does not nap on the Sabbath in order to work better the next day, even to study Torah, for Sabbath rest is for Sabbath enjoyment, not for the sake of a weekday's work.

Sefer Hasidim
13C, #608

NO TASK OTHER THAN BEING HUMAN

Rest in the sense of the traditional Sabbath is quite different from "rest" being defined as not working, or not making an effort (just as "peace" — *shalom* — in the prophetic tradition is more than merely the absence of war; it expresses harmony, wholeness). On the Sabbath, man ceases completely to be an animal whose main occupation is to fight for survival and to sustain his biological life. On the Sabbath, man is fully man, with no task other than to be human.

Erich Fromm
Forgotten Language

SABBATH THE QUEEN

Hayyim Nahman Bialik
(Translated from the Hebrew by I.M. Lask)

The sun o'er the treetops is no longer seen;
Come, let us go forth to greet Sabbath the Queen!
Behold her descending, the holy and blest,
And with her the angels of peace and of rest.
>Welcome, O Queen, welcome!
>Enter thou, enter, O Bride!
Unto you be there peace, ye angels of peace.

The Sabbath is greeted with song and with praise,
We go slowly homewards, our hearts full of grace.
The table is spread there, the candles give light,
Every nook in the house is shining and bright.
>Sabbath is peace and rest.
>Sabbath is peaceful and blest
Enter in peace, ye angels of peace.

O pure one, be with us and light with thy ray
The night and the day, then go on thy way,
And we do thee honor with garments most fine,
With songs and with psalms and with three feasts with wine.
>And by sweetest peace,
>And by perfect peace.
Bless us in peace, ye angels of peace!

The sun in the treetops is no longer seen,
Come forth; we will speed our Sabbath the Queen,
Go thou in peace, our holy and pure one!
Know that for six days we wait you, our sure one!
>Thus for the coming Sabbath,
>Thus for the coming Sabbath!
Pass forth in peace, ye angels of peace.

Abraham E. Millgram
Sabbath Day of Delight

ON *SHABBAT* WE ARE REMINDED

There are days
when we seek things for ourselves and measure failure by
what we do not gain.

On *Shabbat*
we seek not to acquire but to share.

There are days
when we exploit nature as if it were a horn of plenty that can
never be exhausted.

On *Shabbat*
we stand in wonder before the mystery of creation.

There are days
when we act as if we cared nothing for the rights of others.

On *Shabbat*
we are reminded that justice is our duty and a better world our goal.

Therefore we welcome *Shabbat* —

Day of rest,
day of wonder,
day of peace.

Author Unknown

FREE FROM THE CHAINS

The Sabbath is the day of peace between man and nature.... By not working, by not participating in the process of natural and social change — man is free from the chains of nature and from the chains of time, although only for one day a week.

Erich Fromm
The Forgotten Language

PEACEFUL HOURS

This is the meaning of the Jewish Sabbath, to give to man peaceful hours, hours completely diverted from everyday life, seclusion from the world in the midst of the world.

Leo Baeck
The Essence of Judaism

COME SERENELY TO A HALT

A wise non-Jew, Lewis Mumford, wrote "In our Western culture the day of rest has now become another day of busy work, filled with amusements and restless diversions not essentially different from the routine of the work week, particularly in America. From the Sunday morning scramble through the metropolitan newspapers, to the distracting tedium of the motor car excursion, we continuously activate leisure time, instead of letting all work and routine duties come serenely to a halt."

How many can in the midst of all their pressing obligations and commitments, their worries and concerns, business and personal, social or otherwise — just stop everything and say: "I have so many things to do. Now I do nothing. For the next 24 hours, I am a free man. I cut myself off from the world, and all its concerns and limit myself to my home." How many can deliberately and consciously say — not "I have finished, therefore I can rest" — but "though I have not finished, I now stop — there is no such thing as *must* do."

The Sabbath observer can and does. He has no taskmasters. For twenty-four hours he is free. Nothing interferes with his rest, his tranquillity of mind and of soul, unless it be a matter of life and death in which he must play a decisive role. It is not only a matter of not working physically. It is also not working emotionally. And from the positive side, it is the engendering of a completely new and different spirit. Our tradition refers to it as the *neshama y'tairah*, the additional soul. This is an attitude, a state of mind.

Hayim Donin
Beyond Thyself

STOP THE WORLD

To some extent, *Shabbat* achieves what the song title suggests: "Stop the World, I Want to Get Off." Let me paraphrase the Biblical injunction, as it speaks to me, a contemporary person:

Six days shall you be a workaholic; on the seventh day, shall you join the serene company of human beings.

Six days shall you take orders from your boss; on the seventh day shall you be master/mistress of your own life.

Six days shall you toil in the market; on the seventh day, shall you detach from money matters.

Six days shall you create, drive, create, invent, push, drive; on the seventh day, shall you reflect.

Six days shall you be the perfect success; on the seventh day, shall you remember that not everything is in your power.

Six days shall you be a miserable failure; on the seventh day, shall you be on top of the world.

Six days shall you enjoy the blessings of work; on the seventh day, shall you understand that being is as important as doing.

Blu Greenberg
How To Run A Traditional Jewish Household

HOW THE SABBATH DIFFERS

Pre-Israelite versions of Sabbath did not extend the provisions for rest to domestic animals, or to strangers and sojourners temporarily resident in someone's house. They probably did not apply to women either. The Hebrew Sabbath ordinance, on the other hand, is universal. Everyone, including animals, slaves and guests, must stop work. There is no elitism. In the Orient, on the other hand, meditation is practiced mostly by a privileged, partially leisured class. The vast majority of Buddhists in the world do not meditate. They pray or chant on occasion. Meditation is left mostly to the monks. In fact, in most cultures, East and West, prayer and meditation are turned over to a special elite. But this approach presupposes a society where some people work while others meditate — not a very democratic form of spiritual discipline. Such elitism has also dogged the history of Western monasticism, which is Christianity's way of coping with the clash between the *via activa* and the *via contemplativa*. Some people worked while others prayed. For the Jews, however, there was no such spiritual elite. On the Sabbath everyone stopped and just sat.

Sabbath differs from meditation in another way. Not only is it universal, rather than elitist, it is also ethical. For Zen disciples, "just sitting" has no ethical significance whatever, at least not from a Western perspective in which distinguishing good, less good, and evil possibilities is important. In the Sabbath practice, on the other hand, the loftiest of all realities, God himself, is linked to the human needs of the lowest bonded servant. The link is a rare Hebrew verb ("to rest") found only twice in the entire Bible. It means, as we have seen, "to draw one's breath." Both Yahweh and the exhausted slave need to stop and catch their breath, to look up from the task at hand. As the sovereign of the universe, Yahweh can presumably pause whenever he chooses. But the kitchen slave and the grape picker must be protected by divine law from the greed and insensitivity of the rich. The Sabbath discipline is not just an option. It is a legal mandate in order to insure the extension of its full benefits to the poor and the powerless. One ancient version of the Sabbath rule underlines its seriousness by imposing the death penalty on anyone who works or who makes someone else work on Sabbath.

Harvey Cox
Turning East

ON *SHABBAT* WE ARE "AT HOME"

We know from the story of Creation that God "rested" on the seventh day and sanctified it. There, the Hebrew stem *sh-b-t* is used as a verb. Here, in Exodus 16:21-30, it appears as a noun. The Israelites are told to collect a double portion of manna on the sixth day, for the seventh day is "a day of rest, a holy Sabbath of the Lord" when no manna will fall. To this day, then, remembering this injunction, Jews set two whole loaves of *challah* on the Sabbath table.

Naturally, some of the people went out to gather on the seventh day and found nothing. Whereupon God repeats: "Mark that the Lord has given you the Sabbath. Therefore, God gave you two days' food on the sixth day. Let everyone remain where he is: Let no one leave his place on the seventh day." From this point on the Sabbath becomes a fixed institution in Jewish life.

It is no accident, I believe, that the Sabbath is instituted in the context of one of our most intuitively human sources of tension, the concern about having sufficient food to put on our tables. No other concern is as endemic to our human situation. No other concern so completely captures the essence of our struggle to survive on this earth.

But in the midst of this struggle, we are commanded to set aside each seventh day, to withdraw from that struggle, and to rest. And, in the context of this story of manna, the biblical message seems to be that this readiness to withdraw from the struggle for survival on every seventh day becomes one of our most powerful affirmations of faith in God.

Our tradition relates the Sabbath to three distinct moments in time. It is, first, a memorial to the work of Creation; second, a remembrance of the Exodus from Egypt; and finally, a foretaste of *olam habah*, the messianic era. The reference to our redemption from Egypt is clear. Only people who are free can choose not to work. A slave is not the master of his schedule. Our decision, then, to rest on the Sabbath is testimony to our freedom.

But the other two references — to Creation and to the messianic age — are more intricate.

It was the late psychoanalyst Erich Fromm, who in "The Forgotten Language" notes that the prohibition against labor on the Sabbath does not refer to work as we commonly understand it. If it were, why should we be forbidden to carry a handkerchief into the street on the Sabbath? Instead, Fromm suggests, what is forbidden is a creative interference with the natural order. On the Sabbath, we return creation to God.

The Sabbath is a celebration of creation in its most perfect state, the moment when God looked out upon all that had been created and pronounced it "very good." God created a world in which there was perfect harmony between humanity and nature, and the symbol of that state of original harmony was the Sabbath. Never again was the world as perfect as it was at that moment. After the expulsion from Eden, after the beginning of history as we know it, tension enters into the world — tension between people and animals and between people and the earth. Humanity is condemned to wander the earth and to struggle for subsistence — the very struggle we are commanded to relinquish on each Sabbath day.

But we are also promised that this celebration of harmony is also an anticipation of the messianic era when that perfect harmony will be restored forever. For in Jewish eschatology, the end is invariably a recapitulation of the beginning. At the end of days, then, we will be privileged to enjoy, in the words of our tradition, "*yom shekulo Shabbat*," an eternal Sabbath.

That is why we are commanded not to leave our "place" on the Sabbath. Our place, of course, is not literally our houses or our homes. It is rather, metaphorically, our natural place in the cosmos. On the Sabbath day, however briefly, we no longer feel exiled, we no longer are wandering, vulnerable and insecure. Instead, we are all "at home."

More than any other institution, the Sabbath has to be lived to be understood. The experience of this "palace in time" (as it was so felicitously dubbed by Abraham Joshua Heschel) is the most powerful confirmation of the Torah's message that not only is the Sabbath itself an affirmation of God, it is even more a pathway to that affirmation.

Shabbat shalom.

Neil Gillman
The Jewish Week

THE DAY OF COMPLETE HARMONY

The Sabbath is the day of complete harmony between man and nature. "Work" is any kind of disturbance of the man-nature equilibrium. On the basis of this general definition, we can understand the Sabbath ritual.... The Sabbath symbolizes a state of union between man and nature and between man and man. By not working — that is to say, by not participating in the process of natural and social change — man is free from the chains of time.

Erich Fromm
The Forgotten Language

THE BIBLICAL EQUIVALENT OF MEDITATION

The spirit of Sabbath is a biblical equivalent of meditation. It nurtures the same kind of awareness that meditation nurtures, for Sabbath is not just a day for doing nothing. It is a particular form of consciousness, a way of thinking and being that strongly resembles what the Buddhists call "mindfulness."

Harvey Cox
Turning East

WE NEED A DAY OF REST

Judaism has a strong bias in favor of the active and social life. It teaches that God is to be encountered in the world, not in escape from it. But Judaism, of course knows of the great virtues of serenity. The name for the Sabbath in traditional Jewish literature is *yom menuhah,* "a day of rest."

The tempo of modern life is such that man can find neither his God nor himself, except with the utmost effort, amid its distractions. Only through the day of rest, involving a complete cessation from the manipulation of the material world, can man come to know life in its spiritual depths. Judaism does not encourage us to see man's weekday pursuits as a mad and futile scramble but there is a spiritual wholesomeness in a periodic acknowledgment of the ridiculous element in man's ceaseless preoccupation with means rather than with ends.

Louis Jacobs
Faith

A "FANTASTIC" IDEA

James Truslow Adams, the American historian, wrote: "Perhaps it would be a good idea, fantastic as it sounds, to muffle every telephone, halt every motor, and stop all activity some day, to give people a chance to ponder for a few minutes on what it is all about, why they are living and what they really want."

Adams might have been surprised to learn that this "good idea" is not at all "fantastic." Long ago this idea was incorporated in a day which comes every week. We call it *"Shabbat."*

Sidney Greenberg

A FAMILY EXPERIENCE

What happens in my family during the week is probably typical. Breakfast is a five or ten minute affair, and we often do not even eat it together. For lunch we are usually away from home at our various places of work or school. We manage to have dinner together most days, but members of the family are often concerned about what they have to do after dinner, so we often spend as little as fifteen minutes together then. We try to use Sunday afternoons for family outings, but even then the personal calendars of various members of the family sometimes interfere.

Shabbat is different. The rules of the day prohibit many of the activities to which we are running during the rest of the week, and so nobody has to leave. The Friday evening meal lasts for an hour or two, during which we finally get a chance to talk, sing together, and just enjoy each other's company. That kind of family experience continues on Saturday, when various members of the family play games together, take walks, and talk. It is a time when we really get to know each other.

In our day, the car and television set have done a great deal to limit the time that families have to spend together. The car enables us to get from place to place with ease, but that means that we are frequently on the move and away from home. When we are at home we often watch television, during which time there is very little family interaction. In fact, television has a way of closing off discussion because people do not want to have the program interrupted. As a result, members of a family often become strangers to each other. In this context the Sabbath provides a rare opportunity for family members to keep in touch with each other and enjoy moments together. It is therefore no accident that as children become adults and establish their own homes, some of the warmest and most touching memories they have of their parents' homes and of their own are those times spent around the Sabbath table. That is an experience which no Jew of any age should miss.

Elliot N. Dorff
Knowing God: Jewish Journeys to the Unknowable

THE POINT TO REJOIN JUDAISM

In a lucky group like the American Jewish community, which has its full share of life's good things, and which lives at peace, the change from the weekday to the Sabbath is not quite the long dramatic plunge it was for our forefathers — a plunge from gloom, trouble, penury, and crisis to peaceful and graceful pleasure. Our fathers saved all new clothes, all luxurious food, for the day that honored the Creator. No man was so poor that he did not have the wine, the lights, the twisted loaves, and the bit of meat and fish. The synagogue gave him these things if he could not buy them. The restrictions of the Sabbath again, which seem to tug at every turn of American life, were second nature to our fathers, and had vanished into ordinary reality. One did not do a large number of acts on the seventh day as a modern gentleman does not do a large number of acts on any day. But they were so familiar that they were the very air of life rather than self-consciously executed disciplines. There was no grain for them to go against. They were the grain.

The American Jew, by taking thought and pains, by keeping the Sabbath over the years, by accepting its difficulties for the sake of the results, can have what the Sabbath offers. He has to work at it more than his fathers did, with a lower charge of religious energy. It is a hard case. That the Sabbath should be the usual breaking-off point from tradition is perhaps inevitable. It is also the point at which many Jews rejoin Judaism. Probably it is the natural and the best point.

Elliot N. Dorff
Knowing God: Jewish Journeys to the Unknowable

What was created on the Sabbath day after God rested? Peace of mind, rest, contentment, and quiet.

Genesis Rabbah, Ch. 10

HOW GOD COMFORTED THE TORAH

Once the Torah asked, "God of the world, when the people Israel enters the Promised Land, what will become of me? Each Israelite will be busy with plowing and sowing his field, and what, then, will happen to me?" God answered the Torah, "I have a love partner which I am giving to You. It is *Shabbat.* When Israel ceases working, they will enter synagogues and study places and devote themselves to working with Torah."

Sefer Ha-Agadah 381:22

THE "USELESS" DAY

I view the Sabbath... as a "useless" day. We must once again understand that doing nothing, being silent and open to the world, letting things happen inside, can be as important as, and sometimes more important than, what we commonly call the useful. Let there be some special time during the week when we do for the sake of doing; when we love the trivial and, in fact, simply love; when we do for others rather than ourselves and thus provide a counterbalance for the weight of endless competition that burdens our every day.

W. Gunther Plaut
A Shabbat Manual

AN EVER MORE PRECIOUS RESOURCE FOR LIFE

By and large we modern Jews are not exhausted by physical exertions during our work week. Few of us dig tunnels, unload cargoes, mine coal, man steel furnaces, or operate heavy machinery. We do not go to work by trudging many miles on foot. We have at our disposal the amenities of the automobile, caught in traffic jams, or commuter trains invariably crowded and late, or the buses and subways, of which the less said the better. By the end of the week our muscles are not physically fatigued; instead, our nerves are frayed. Not toil, but tension, is the toll that modern life exacts from us and from our contemporaries. We need rest and surcease, not so much from physical strain as from psychic stress built up during the week.

It is precisely the traditional Sabbath that speaks to our present condition, by enjoining the avoidance of travel, shopping, cooking, and writing, and by limiting our movements to what we can do with our own power, by walking. What the prayer book beautifully describes as *menucha shelema*, "total rest," is only within the power of the traditional Sabbath to bestow. As tensions continue to mount in contemporary society, the traditional Sabbath, that requires an all-but-total separation from work-a-day tasks and concerns and worry, becomes an ever more precious resource for life in a world increasingly dedicated to death.

Robert Gordis
Judaism

10

SHEAF OF SHABBAT
PRAYERS
AND MEDITATIONS

Wolpert, Ludwig. Havdalah Set. JM 39-60. Jewish Museum/Art Resource, New York, U.S.A.

ACCEPT OUR GRATITUDE

For the blessings which You lavish upon us in forest and sea, in mountain and meadow, in rain and sun, we thank You.

For the blessings You implant within us, joy and peace, meditation and laughter, we are grateful to You.

For the blessings of friendship and love, of family and community;

For the blessings we ask of You and those we cannot ask;

For the blessings You bestow upon us openly and those You give us in secret;

For all these blessings, O Lord of the universe, we thank You and are grateful to You.

For the blessings we recognize and those we fail to recognize;

For the blessings of our tradition and of our holy days;

For the blessings of return and forgiveness, of memory, of vision, and of hope;

For all these blessings which surround us on every side, O Lord, hear our thanks and accept our gratitude.

Ruth Brin
as adapted in *Likrat Shabbat*

TO LOVE AND TO CARE

We thank You, O God, for our family and for what we mean and bring to one another. We are grateful for the bonds of loyalty and affection which sustain us, and which keep us close to one another no matter how far apart we may be.

We thank You for implanting within us a deep need for each other, and for giving us the capacity to love and to care.

Help us to be modest in our demands of one another, but generous in our giving to each other. May we never measure how much love or encouragement we offer; may we never count the times we forgive. Rather, may we always be grateful that we have one another and that we are able to express our love in acts of kindness.

Keep us gentle in our speech. When we offer words of criticism, may they be chosen with care and spoken softly. May we waste no opportunity to speak words of sympathy, of appreciation, of praise.

Bless our family with health, happiness, and contentment. Above all, grant us the wisdom to build a joyous and peaceful home in which Your spirit will always abide.

Amen.

Sidney Greenberg
Likrat Shabbat

THE WONDROUS REWARDS OF KEEPING *SHABBAT*

Shabbat Musaf:
You ordained *Shabbat*, You willed her holy intimacy, You inspired her symbols, rites, profundities. Jews who rejoice on *Shabbat* reap everlasting glory. Jews who cherish *Shabbat* gain fullness of life. Jews who reassure her subtlest details choose a legacy of grandeur. Ever since Sinai we bear this honor and obey God's command to celebrate *Shabbat*....

Those who observe *Shabbat*, calling it a pleasure, rejoice in Your sovereignty. Contentment and delight with Your blessings, fill all who keep *Shabbat* holy, the seventh day, Your will and mystery and joy, sweetest of days, memento of Creation.

Andre Ungar
Siddur Sim Shalom

THE GIFTS WE PRAY FOR

Our God and God of our ancestors, accept our *Shabbat* offering of rest. Add holiness to our lives with Your *mitzvot* and let Your Torah be our portion. Fill our lives with Your goodness, and gladden us with Your triumph. Cleanse our hearts and we shall serve You faithfully, Lovingly and willingly, Lord our God, grant that we inherit Your holy gift of *Shabbat* forever, so that Your people Israel who hallow your name will always find rest on this day. Praised are You, Lord who hallows *Shabbat*.

From *Shabbat* morning *Amidah*
Translation by Jules Harlow
Siddur Sim Shalom

MEDITATIONS BEFORE *KIDDUSH*

On this Sabbath, which is a reminder of creation,
We thank You, O God, for the world which You created.

You have filled Your world with beauty for our eyes,
With music and laughter for our ears,
With soft things for us to touch,
With fragrances for us to smell,
With fine foods to sustain us and to bring us delight.

As we enjoy the many blessings
Which You have so bountifully granted,
May we, too, bring goodness into the lives of others.

As we recall Your blessings,
Too many to be counted, too constant to be merited,
May we be moved to thank You always, as we do now,
For the fruit of the vine which You have created
And for the *Shabbat* which You have sanctified.

Sidney Greenberg
Likrat Shabbat

MEDITATIONS FOR SABBATH CANDLE LIGHTING

I

Gracious God, thank You for the privilege of ushering in another *Shabbat* of rest and peace.

With a full heart, I thank You for the blessings of the week which has passed, and for the strength which I was granted to overcome its difficulties.

I ask Your blessings for the week that lies ahead. Grant health and contentment to my loved ones and friends. Help us to strengthen each other with gentle words and acts of kindness. Bestow Your blessings upon all Your children.

May this home be a sacred shrine in which You will delight to dwell.

Amen.

II

May the brightness of these candles banish all gloom, anxiety, and care from my heart and from the hearts of my loved ones.

May this *Shabbat* bring us peace and serenity, joy and rest. Keep aglow within us, O God, the spirit of gratitude for Your many blessings, so that we may know the sweet taste of contentment and the rich harvest of sharing.

Kindle in our home a deeper love for one another, for our people, and for all Your children.

Amen.

Sidney Greenberg
Likrat Shabbat

A CROWNING GRACE

Shabbat Afternoon:
You are One, Your name, "The One." What nation, though scattered on earth, is One as is Your people Israel? To us, Your people, You gave an infinite beauty, a crowning grace; a day of rest and holiness. Abraham made merry on it, Isaac sang aloud on it, Jacob found peace on it, and so do we, their offspring. Tranquil with love and freedom are we, tranquil with truth and faith, tranquil with peace and calm, with quiet and safety, altogether serene, worthy of You. May we, Your children, sense and see that as our peace flows from You so must our gratitude stream to You.

Andre Ungar
Siddur Sim Shalom

SHABBAT'S LIBERATING JOY

Grant me the privilege of the liberating joy of *Shabbat*, the privilege of truly tasting the delight of *Shabbat*. May I be undisturbed by sadness, by sorrow, or by sighing during the holy hours of *Shabbat*. Fill Your servant's heart with joy, for to You, O Lord, I offer my entire being. Let me hear joy and jubilation. Help me to expand the dimensions of all *Shabbat* delights. Help me to extend the joy of *Shabbat* to the other days of the week, until I attain the goal of deep joy always. Show me the path of life, the full joy of Your Presence, the bliss of being close to You forever. May the words of my mouth and the meditations of my heart be acceptable to You, O Lord, my Rock and my Redeemer.

Jules Harlow
Siddur Sim Shalom

FOR MY FAMILY

Avinu malkeinu, bless my family with peace. Teach us to appreciate the treasure of our lives. Help us always to find contentment in one another. Save us from dissension and jealousy; shield us from pettiness and rivalry. May selfish pride not divide us; may pride in one another unite us. Help us to renew our love for one another continually. In the light of Your Torah grant us, the people Israel and all Your creatures everywhere, health and fulfillment, harmony, peace, and joy. Amen.

Translation by Navah Harlow
Siddur Sim Shalom

THE PROFOUND MEANING OF BEING AT ONE

A vision of *Shabbat,* an insight into the profound meaning of being at One: Through the service of *Kabbalat Shabbat,* the throne of glory is prepared for the holy King. With the arrival of *Shabbat,* the *Shekhinah* is liberated from all forces of evil and harsh judgments, leaving her free for intimate union with the holy light, adorned with many crowns by the holy King. All kingdoms of anger, all dominions of judgment, flee from her presence; no alien power reigns in all the universe. She is bathed in light from on high while receiving a crown of *Shabbat* prayers from earth, from the holy people, all of whom are adorned with the fresh additional souls which are theirs on *Shabbat.* Then they begin *Shabbat* prayers, happily blessing her, joy and gladness on every face, released from thoughts of severity and judgment, uttering *Barkhu,* "Praise the Lord," as *Shabbat* blessings and peace begin to flow.

Zohar, Terumah
Translation by Jules Harlow
Siddur Sim Shalom

HOW DOES *SHABBAT* BLESS US?
LET US COUNT THE WAYS

Shabbat celebrates the world's creation.

On *Shabbat* we attest that God is Creator;
blessed are those who tell of His goodness.

Shabbat expands our lives with holiness

Be open to joy with both body and soul
blessed are those who make *Shabbat* a delight.

Shabbat is a foretaste of future redemption.

Rejoice in *Shabbat*, inherit God's holy mountain;
blessed are those who will sing in His Temple.
The homeless will all be restored to His home.

Shabbat rest makes whole our fragmented lives.

It foreshadows a world which is totally peace.
Blessed be God, the Master of peace;
may His harmony, seen in nature, enhance ever life.

May we be renewed by the calm of *Shabbat*,
as we praise our Creator for the gift of *Shabbat*.

Siddur Sim Shalom

HOW DOES *SHABBAT* BLESS US?
LET US COUNT THE WAYS

To celebrate *Shabbat* is to share in holiness;

the presence of eternity, a moment of majesty,
the radiance of joy, enhancement of the soul.

To celebrate *Shabbat* is to realize freedom.

Shabbat reminds us that we are all royalty,
that all mortals are equal, children of God.

To celebrate *Shabbat* is to surpass limitations.

We can sanctify time and redeem history,
affirm the world without becoming its slaves.

To celebrate *Shabbat* is to sing its melody.

We delight in the song of the spirit, the joys of the good,
the grandeur of living in the face of eternity.

To celebrate *Shabbat* is to sense God's Presence.

He sustains us even when our spirits falter.
may we deepen our spirituality and expand our compassion
as we praise our Creator for the holiness of *Shabbat*.

Based on words by Abraham Joshua Heschel
Siddur Sim Shalom

THE *SHABBAT*

This is the great warmth, the great at-homeness;
This is the knowledge of belonging;
The loneness merging into a strong oneness.
One lost drop of water finding its way into the sea.

The Torah gleams white and silver, and we stand
Signing and praying.
Our hearts warm with peace.
Our spirits quiet in the quietness of *Shabbat*.

This is the end of the week and its beginning.
This is the moment of pause,
The refilling of the empty vessel,
The renewing of the spirit.

This is the remembering;
The shared memory of two thousand years
And the shared embarking upon two thousand more.

This is the hearth, the gathering together;
The pain and the joy,
The tears and the gentle laughter.

This is the benign wisdom in an old man's eyes
And the hope in a child's fresh voice.
The roots into the past
And the arms stretched forward into the future.

E. Grindell
The Reconstructionist
as adapted in *Likrat Shabbat*

ACKNOWLEDGMENTS
AND NOTES

P. 2   *How a Sweatshop*...by Sidney Greenberg, from <u>Lessons for Living</u>. Copyright © 1985. With permission of Hartmore House.

P. 3   *An Island of Stillness.* Excerpt from "Beyond Civilization" from <u>The Sabbath</u> by Abraham Joshua Heschel. Copyright © 1951 by Abraham Joshua Heschel. Copyright renewed © 1979 by Sylvia Heschel. Repriinted by permission of Farrar, Strauss & Giroux, Inc.

P. 4   *God's Most Precious*...From <u>Our Jewish Heritage</u> by Joseph Gaer and Alfred Wolf. With permission of Henry Holt and Co.

P. 4   *Life is Worthwhile.* Adapted from Mordecai M. Kaplan.

P. 5   *A Sure Fire Prescription.* From <u>Beyond Thyself</u> by Hayim Donin. With permission of Charles Bloch Co. Publishers.

P. 5   *Shabbat Unifies*...From <u>The Jewish Way — Living the Holidays</u>, p. 141, by Irving Greenberg. Copyright © 1988, Summit Publishers.

P. 5   *Shabbat Nurtures*...From <u>A Jewish Philosophy and Pattern of Life</u> by Simon Greenberg. Published by The Jewish Theological Seminary of America. Copyright © 1981. Reprinted by permission.

P. 6   *A Day for the Body*...From <u>The Sabbath</u>, p. 52, by Samuel H. Dresner. Copyright © 1970. With permission of Burning Bush Press.

P. 6   *Preparing For*...From the <u>Shulhan Aruh</u> by Joseph Caro.

P. 7   *Taking Time Out.* From <u>Everything But Money</u> by Samuel Levenson. Reprinted by permission of Sterling Lord Literistic, Inc. Copyright © by Samuel Levenson.

P. 7   *Rest and Grow.* By Sidney Greenberg.

P. 7   *Shabbat — A Gift from God.* By Elliot B. Gertel.

P. 8   *Why is the Sabbath*...From <u>The Sabbath</u>, p. 17, by Samuel H. Dresner. Copyright © 1970. With permission of Burning Bush Press.

P. 8   *Shabbat — A Sample.* From "Otiyot d'Rabbi Akiva" as adapted in <u>Likrat Shabbat</u>. Edited by Sidney Greenberg and Jonathan D. Levine © 1992 & 1973 by The Prayer Book Press of Media Judaica.

P. 9   *Welcome to the Bride.* From <u>The Sabbath,</u> p. 19, by Samuel H. Dresner. Copyright © 1970. With permission of Burning Bush Press.

P. 9   *Shabbat's Mate.* From <u>Genesis Rabbah</u> 11:8.

P. 10 *Beyond Creation and Revelation.* From <u>Franz Rosenzweig:</u>
<u>His Life and Thought</u> by Nahum Glatzer, Schocken
Books, Inc. Copyright © 1953.

P. 10 *The First Step*...From <u>Die Religion der Vernuft</u> by Hermann
Cohen.

P. 11 *The Sabbath — Our Goal.* From <u>East River</u> by Sholem Asch,
Copyright ©1946. Carrol Graf Publishers.

P. 11 *What Shabbat Does for Us.* By Sidney Greenberg from <u>Siddur</u>
<u>Hadash</u>. Edited by Sidney Greenberg and Jonathan D. Levine
© 1992 & 1973 by The Prayer Book Press of Media Judaica.

P. 12 *A Weekly Gift.* By Sidney Greenberg.

P. 12 *Shabbat Reminds us*...Central Conference of American Rabbis:
from <u>Gates of Shabbat</u> by Mark Dov Shapiro. Copyright ©
1991. CCAR Press. Used with permission.

P. 12 *We Can Consecrate*...From <u>In God's Mirror</u> by Harold
Schulweis, Ktav Publishing House. Copyright © 1990, author
of <u>For Those Who Can't Believe</u>, HarperCollins.

P. 14 *The Shabbat Has Kept Us Alive.* By Ahad Ha'am.

P. 14 *When Shabbat Laws*...From <u>Mishneh Torah,</u> Hilkhot Shabbat
11:5, by Moses Maimonides.

P. 14 *Some Business*... From the <u>Babylonian Talmud,</u> Shabbat 150a.

P. 15 *Shabbat — Good for the Heart.* By Sidney Greenberg.

P. 15 *Enjoying the Richness*...By Jacob J. Staub in <u>The Jewish</u>
<u>Exponent</u>, Aug. 7, 1992.

P. 16 *A Hidden Treasure.* Reprinted from "Sabbath: A Hasidic
Dimension" by Pinhas Peli in <u>Perspectives In Jews and</u>
<u>Judaism: Essays in Honor of Wolfe Kelman</u>. Edited by Rabbi
Arthur A. Chiel. Copyright © 1978 by the Rabbinical
Assembly. Reprinted by permission of the Rabbinical
Assembly.

P. 18 *The Spice of the Feast.* From the <u>Babylonian Talmud,</u>
Shabbat 119a.

P. 18 *Shabbat Sweetens*...By Louis Jacobs from <u>Great Jewish Ideas,</u>
Edited by Abraham Millgram. Copyright © 1964. With
permission of B'nai B'rith International Commission on
Continuing Jewish Education.

P. 18 *Sacred Duties*...From <u>Joy and Remembrance</u> by Max Arzt.
Copyright © 1979. With permission of Hartmore House.

P. 19 *The Arrival*... from the <u>Babylonian Talmud,</u> Shabbat 119a.

P. 19 *A Mother's Shabbat Prayer.* Reprinted from <u>Siddur Sim</u>
<u>Shalom,</u> edited with translations by Rabbi Jules Harlow.
Published by The Rabbinical Assembly and The United
Synagogue of Conservative Judaism. Copyright 1985 by The
Rabbinical Assembly. Reprinted by permission.

P. 20 *The Shabbat Brings*...From <u>The Sabbath</u>, p. 48, by Samuel H.

Dresner. Copyright © 1970. With permission of Burning Bush
Press.

P. 20   *Be Quick...*From <u>Yesod v'Shoresh ha-Avodah</u> by Alexander
         Susskind.

P. 21   *Blessed is the Match.* By Hannah Senesh. Translation from a
         brochure by United Synagogue of Conservative Judaism.

P. 21   *Sabbath and the Kitchen Girls.* From "Esser Tzachtzochoth" by
         I. Berger in the <u>Hasidic Anthology</u> by Louis I. Newman.
         Bloch Pub. Co. Copyright © 1934.

P. 21   *Whom Shabbat Honors.* From the <u>Shulhan Aruh</u> by Joseph
         Caro.

P. 22   *Making Shabbes.* From <u>The Art of Jewish Living — The
         Shabbat Seder</u> by Ron Wolfson. With permission of the
         Federation of Jewish Men's Clubs.

P. 22   *Rich Values...*From<u> A Guide to the Sabbath</u> by Solomon
         Goldman © Jewish Chronicle Publications. Distributed by
         Hartmore House.

P. 23   *"Shabbat" Instead of Saturday."* By Sidney Greenberg.

P. 23   *Judaism Begins in the Home.* By Morris Adler.

P. 24   *The Mother's Tears.* From <u>Lithuania of My Birth</u> by Abraham
         Kariv. Copyright © 1967. With permission of Herzl Press.

P. 24   *A Choice* from <u>Living a Jewish Life,</u> by Anita Diamant and
         Howard Cooper. Copyright © 1991 by Anita Diamant and
         Howard Cooper. HarperCollins Publishers.

P. 25   *Restorative Magic.* From <u>This is My God</u> by Herman Wouk.
         Copyright © 1959 by the Abe Wouk Foundation, Inc.
         Copyright © renewed 1987 by Herman Wouk. By permission
         of Little, Brown and Company.

P. 26   *The Binding Glue For the Family.* By Sidney Greenberg.

P. 27   *We Must Convert Saturday to Shabbat.* By Sidney Greenberg.

P. 28   *Tzedakah — A Jewish Passion.* From <u>The Art of Jewish
         Living — The Shabbat Seder</u> by Ron Wolfson. With
         permission of the Federation of Jewish Men's Clubs.

P. 28   *A Chance Truly to Rest.* Translated from the Yiddish by
         Arthur Green in <u>The First Jewish Catalog</u> by Richard Siegel
         and Michael and Sharon Strassfeld. Copyright © 1973.
         With permission of The Jewish Publication Society.

P. 29   *How Does Wine...*from <u>Gates of Shabbat</u> by Mark Dov
         Shapiro. Copyright ©1991. CCAR Press. Used with
         permission.

P. 30   *Why is the Challah...*from <u>Gates of Shabbat</u> by Mark Dov
         Shapiro. Copyright © 1991. CCAR Press. Used with
         permission.

P. 30   *Why Are Two Loaves Used?* from _Gates of Shabbat_ by Mark
         Dov Shapiro. Copyright © 1991. CCAR Press. Used with
         permission.

P. 31   *Sabbath — A Sign of Eternity*. From _Sabbath Day of Eternity_
         by Aryeh Kaplan. Copyright © 1974 by Aryeh Kaplan. New
         Edition, copyright © 1982. Reprinted with permission of
         Orthodox Union/ National Conference of Synagogue Youth.

P. 31   *A Day Speaks*...From _Essence of Judaism_ by Leo Baeck.
         Schocken Books, Copyright © 1948.

P. 32   *On A Clear Shabbat*...By Lawrence Hoffman in _The Jewish
         Week_, reprinted with the permission of _The Jewish Week_.

P. 34   *Consecration*...From _The Jewish Sabbath_ by Pinhas Peli,
         Pantheon Books. Copyright © 1991. With permission of
         Pantheon Books.

P. 35   *Symbol of Our Higher Destiny*. From "Leisure And the
         Church" in _Religion in a Changing World_ by Abba Hillel Silver.
         NY: R.R. Smith, Copyright © 1930.

P. 35   *The Cornerstone*...From _Sefer Ha-Shabbat_ by Hayyim Nahman
         Bialik.

P. 36   *Keep As Much*...By M. Friedlander.

P. 36   *Israel's Mate*. From _Genesis Rabbah_ 11:8.

P. 37   *A Litmus Test*... From _Knowing God: Jewish Journeys to the
         Unknowable_ by Elliot N. Dorff. Reprinted with the
         permission of Jason Aronson Inc., Northvale, NJ. Copyright ©
         1992.

P. 37   *The Great Educator* From _Pentateuch and Haftorahs_ by
         Joseph H. Hertz. Copyright © 1968. With permission of The
         Soncino Press LTD.

P. 38   *How To Express Joy*. From the _Babylonian Talmud_, Shabbat
         118b.

P. 38   *The Whole Person*...From _God, Man and History_ by Eliezer
         Berkovits. Copyright © 1959. With permission of Jonathan
         David Publishers.

P. 39   *A Taste of Perfection*. From _Seeking the Path to Life_ by Ira F.
         Stone. Woodstock, VT: Jewish Lights Publishing. Copyright ©
         1992. $19.95 (hc) + $3.00 s/h each book. Order by mail or
         call 800-962-4544. Permission granted by Jewish Lights
         Publishing, PO Box 237, Woodstock, VT 05091.

P. 40   *We Are Co-Sanctifiers* From _In God's Mirror_ by Harold
         Schulweis, Ktav Publishing House. Copyright © 1990, author
         of _For Those Who Can't Believe_, HarperCollins.

P. 40   *The Reservoir*...By Natan Scharansky.

P. 41   *They Didn't Know*. From _Influences of the Old Testament on
         Puritanism_ by William Selbie.

P. 41   *To Live*...By Arnold Jacob Wolf. from <u>Gates of Shabbat</u> by
         Mark Dov Shapiro. Copyright © 1991. CCAR Press. Used with
         permission.

P. 41   *How Long is a Week?* By Sidney Greenberg.

P. 42   *An Exquisite*...From <u>Seek My face, Speak My Name</u> by Arthur
         Green. Copyright © 1992. With permission of Jason
         Aronson, Inc.

P. 43   *Day of Delight.* From <u>The Book of Jewish Practices</u> by Louis
         Jacobs. Published by Behrman House, Inc. 235 Watchung
         Ave. W. Orange. NJ 07052. Used with permission.

P. 44   *We Must Prepare*...From <u>The Book of the Pious</u> by Judah the
         Pious.

P. 45   *A Bit of Shabbat*...From <u>Noam Elimelech</u> by Elimelech of
         Lizensk

P. 45   *Henrietta Szold's Strength.* By Sidney Greenberg.

P. 45   *The Sabbath is*...From the <u>Zohar</u>, Genesis 48a.

P. 46   *It May Save Us*...By Alexander M. Shapiro.

P. 46   *A Messianic Celebration.* By Steven S. Schwarzschild from
         <u>Great Jewish Ideas</u>, Edited by Abraham Millgram, Copyright ©
         1964. With permission of B'nai B'rith International
         Commission on Continuing Jewish Education.

P. 47   <u>A Weekly Truce.</u> By Harold Kushner.

P. 47   *Learn By Living It.* From <u>Sabbath Day of Eternity</u> by
         Aryeh Kaplan. Copyright © 1974 by Aryeh Kaplan. New
         Edition, Copyright © 1982. Reprinted with permission of
         Orthodox Union/ National Conference of Synagogue Youth.

P. 48   *Making Shabbat Special.* Excerpted from an article in the
         <u>United Synagogue Review</u>, Volume 44, No. 2, Spring.
         Copyright © 1992. Reprinted with permission.

P. 50   *The Joys of Shabbat.* By Sidney Greenberg in <u>Siddur Hadash</u>.
         Edited by Sidney Greenberg and Jonathan D. Levine © 1992
         by The Prayer Book Press of Media Judaica.

P. 51   *To Drink Life Deeply.* By Sandy Eisenberg Sasso in <u>Kol
         Haneshamah</u>. With permission of Federation of
         Reconstructionist Congregations and Havurot.

P. 51   *A Blessing in Itself.* By Jane Epstein in <u>Your Child</u>, Vol XXII,
         No. 3. With permission of United Synagogue of Conservative
         Judaism., Commission on Jewish Education.

P. 52   *Our Part of the Bargain.* By Elliot B. Gertel.

P. 55   *A Palace in Time.* Excerpt from "Beyond Civilization" from
         <u>The Sabbath</u> by Abraham Joshua Heschel. Copyright © 1951
         by Abraham Joshua Heschel. Copyright renewed © 1979 by

Sylvia Heschel. Reprinted by permission of Farrar, Strauss& Giroux, Inc.

P. 56 *Roping Off Time.* From <u>How to Run a Traditional Jewish Household</u> by Blu Greenberg. Copyright © 1983 by Blu Greenberg. Reprinted by permission, Simon and Schuster, Inc.

P. 57 *One Word -and Tears.* By Shlomo Riskin, in <u>Hadassah Magazine,</u> April, 1987.

P. 58 *Sabbath Prayer.* By Ruth Brin from <u>Harvest: Collected Poems and Prayers.</u> Reconstructionist Press. Copyright © 1986 by Ruth Brin. Reprinted by permission.

P. 58 *A Day of...*From <u>The Jewish Way of Life</u> by David Aronson. Copyright © 1957. With permission of The National Academy for Adult Jewish Studies, United Synagogue of Conservative Judaism.

P. 59 *Freedom and the Sanctification...*By Ovadiah Sforno.

P. 59 *Embraced By...*From <u>The Book of Jewish Belief</u> by Louis Jacobs, Published by Behrman House, Inc., 235 Watchung Ave., W. Orange, NJ 07052. Copyright ©1984. Used with permission.

P. 60 *The Seed of Eternity...* Excerpt from "Beyond Civilization" from <u>The Sabbath </u>by Abraham Joshua Heschel. Copyright © 1951 by Abraham Joshua Heschel. Copyright renewed ©1979 by Sylvia Heschel. Reprinted by permission of Farrar, Strauss & Giroux, Inc.

P. 60 *When Shabbat...*By Ben Zion Bokser.

P. 60 *The Eternal...* From <u>The Sabbath </u> by Samuel H. Dresner. Copyright © 1970. With permission of Burning Bush Press.

P. 61 *There Is Nothing...*From <u>The Jewish Sabbath</u> by Pinhas Peli, Pantheon Books. Copyright © 1991. With permission of Pantheon Books.

P. 61 *Shabbat-aging.* By Rabbi Stanley Yedwab.

P. 62 *Shabbat Work.* By Shira Milgrom.

P. 63 *Shabbos Has Come.* By Myron Fenster.

P. 64 *Rest Is Freedom.* From <u>Forgotten Language</u> by Erich Fromm, Holt, Rinehart and Winston Pub. Copyright 1951. ©1979 by Erich Fromm. Reprinted by permission of Henry Holt and Co., Inc.

P. 65 *On Shabbat We Come Home.* From <u>The Jewish Sabbath</u> by Pinhas Peli, Pantheon Books. Copyright © 1991. With permission of Pantheon Books.

P. 65 *The Perfect Sabbath...*by Moses Maimonides, from <u>Hebrew Ethical Wills</u>, Tzavah 101, Edited by Israel Abrahams. Jewish Publication Society, Copyright © 1926.

P. 65   *The Holy One*...from <u>Babylonian Talmud</u>, Betza, 16a.

P. 66   *How We Sanctify Time*. By Sidney Greenberg in <u>Minhat Shabbat</u>. Edited by Sidney Greenberg and Jonathan D. Levine © 1995 by The Prayer Book Press of Media Judaica.

P. 67   *Prayer of a Jewish Woman*...Translated from the Yiddish by Arthur Green in <u>The First Jewish Catalog</u> by Richard Siegel and Michael and Sharon Strassfeld. Copyright © 1973. With permission of The Jewish Publication Society.

P. 67   *The Sabbath is*...By Israel Zangwill.

P. 68   *Symbol and Instrument* ...From <u>The Meaning of God in Modern Jewish Religion</u> by Mordecai M. Kaplan. Copyright © 1947. Reconstructionist Press. With permission.

P. 68   *Investing Time*...By Mordecai Waxman.

P. 69   *An Architect of Time*. By Shira Milgrom.

P. 69   *To Stay in Touch*...From <u>Living a Jewish Life</u>, by Anita Diamant and Howard Cooper. Copyright © 1991 by Anita Diamant and Howard Cooper. HarperCollins Publishers. 1992. With permission of Jason Aronson, Inc.

P. 70   *A Day for Renewing Ourselves*. From <u>Knowing God:Jewish Journeys to the Unknowable</u>, by Elliot N. Dorff. Copyright ©1992. With permission of Jason Aaronson.

P. 70   *A New Gift. By* Arthur Green, <u>Reconstructionist Magazine</u>, July, 1991.

P. 71   *Action and Rest*. From <u>Turning East</u> by Harvey Cox. Copyright ©1977 by Harvey Cox. Reprinted by permission of Simon and Schuster, Inc.

P. 72   *A Community Experience*. From <u>Knowing God: Jewish Journeys to the Unknowable</u>, by Elliot N. Dorff. Copyright © 1992. With permission of Jason Aaronson, Inc.

P. 73   *A Short Amidah*. By Sid Lieberman. From <u>Ra'ayonot Magazine.</u>

P. 74   *To Share What is Eternal*... Excerpt from "Beyond Civilization" from <u>The Sabbath </u>by Abraham Joshua Heschel. Copyright © 1951 by Abraham Joshua Heschel. Copyright renewed © 1979 by Sylvia Heschel. Reprinted by permission of Farrar, Strauss & Giroux, Inc.

P. 74   *Longing for*...By Yitzchak Maor in <u>Reconstructionist Magazine.</u>

P. 75   *God, I Have Time* by Michael Quoist. from <u> Gates of Shabbat</u> by Mark Dov Shapiro. Copyright © 1991. CCAR Press. Used with permission.

P. 76   *The Pauses Between the Notes*. By Sidney Greenberg in <u>Likrat Shabbat</u>. Edited by Sidney Greenberg and Jonathan D. Levine © 1992 & 1973 by The Prayer Book Press of Media Judaica.

P. 76   *What Our Sick*...By Rev. Dr. Ernest R. Palen.

P. 77   *Preparing For Shabbat*. By Richard Siegel. Originally appeared in <u>Moment Magazine,</u> January 1976.

P. 78   *In the Forest.* From <u>The Jewish Sabbath</u> by Pinhas Peli.
         Pantheon Books, Copyright © 1991. With permission of
         Pantheon Books.

P. 80   *When We Make It Different.* By Rabbi Ralph Simon, Rabbi
         Emeritus of Congregation Rodfei Zedek, Chicago, Illinois.

P. 81   *Shabbat in the Gulag.* By Yosef Mendelovich, in <u>The Jewish</u>
         <u>Week</u>, 1990. Reprinted with the permission of <u>The Jewish</u>
         <u>Week</u>.

P. 82   *How Are the Candles Lit?* from <u>Gates of Shabbat</u> by Mark Dov
         Shapiro, Copyright © 1991. CCAR Press. Used with
         permission.

P. 82   *In a Nazi Transport.* From <u>Likrat Shabbat</u>. Edited by Sidney
         Greenberg and Jonathan D. Levine © 1992 & 1973 by The
         Prayer Book Press of Media Judaica.

P. 83   *The Sabbath Candles Transformed Us.* From <u>The Search For</u>
         <u>God at Harvard</u> by Ari L. Goldman. Copyright © 1991 by Ari
         L. Goldman. Random House. Reprinted by permission of
         Time Books, A Division of Random House, Inc.

P. 84   *Shabbat Conferred...*By Elie Wiesel, from "To Be a Jew" in <u>A</u>
         <u>Jew Today.</u> Copyright © 1978. Random House Publishers.

P. 84   *The Shabbat I'll Never Forget.* By Deborah Chasan.

P. 85   *In the Shtetl.* From <u>The World of Sholem Aleichem</u> by Maurice
         Samuel. Pantheon Books. Copyright © 1962. With
         permission of Pantheon Books.

P. 86   *My Mother-In-Law's...*From <u>How to Run a Traditional Jewish</u>
         <u>Household</u>, by Blu Greenberg. Copyright © 1983 by Blu
         Greenberg. Reprinted by permission, Simon and Schuster, Inc.

P. 86   *Happy is He...*by S.J. Agnon.

P. 87   *On New York's Lower East Side.* From <u>The Greatest Jewish City</u>
         <u>in the World</u> by Harry Golden. Copyright © 1972. With
         permission of Doubleday Dell Pub. Co.

P. 87   *Why Zaida Cried.* From <u>He Kindled a Light: A Philosophy of</u>
         <u>Jewish Education</u>, by Philip Arian, Ed. by Chaim Picker .
         Copyright © 1976. With permission of United Synagogue of
         Conservative Judaism,

P. 88   *Shabbat Is...*By Andre Ungar.

P. 89   *The Additional Soul* From <u>Lithuania Land of My Birth</u> by
         Avraham Kariv. Copyright © 1967. With permission of Herzl
         Press.

P. 90   *The Sabbath Speaks...*From <u>Judaism: Profile of a Faith</u> by Ben
         Zion Bokser. Copyright © 1963 from Alfred Knopf Co., Inc.
         Reprinted by permission.

P. 91   *The World Is Not Ours.* By Sampson Raphael Hirsch.

P. 91   *The Sabbath has been...*From <u>The Cuzari</u>, by Judah Halevi.

P. 92   *An Essential*...by Israel Meir Kagan, quoted in <u>Saint and Sages</u>
        by Moshe M. Yashar. Copyright © 1937. With permission of
        Charles Bloch Pub. Co.

P. 92   *The Weekly Reminder.* By Louis Jacobs, as adapted in <u>Likrat
        Shabbat</u>. Edited by Sidney Greenberg and Jonathan D. Levine
        © 1992 & 1973 by The Prayer Book Press of Media Judaica.

P. 93   *"Remember"*...From Rabbi Irwin Groner.

P. 93   *To Observe*...From <u>Mekhilta</u> to Exodus, 20.13

P. 94   *Giving Up Control.* From <u>A Living Covenant: The Innovative
        Spirit in Traditional Judaism</u> by David Hartman. Copyright ©
        1985 by Free Press, a Division of Simon and Schuster.
        Reprinted with the permission of the publisher.

P. 95   *Not Masters.* By Immanuel Jakobovitz in "Jewish Law Faces
        Modern Problems" published in <u>Studies in Modern Judaism</u>,
        edited by Leon Stitskin.

P. 95   *Higher Than*...By C.G. Montefiore. as adapted in <u>Likrat
        Shabbat</u> . Edited by Sidney Greenberg and Jonathan D. Levine
        © 1992 & 1973 by The Prayer Book Press of Media Judaica.

P. 96   *Saved From*...From <u>The Jewish Sabbath</u> by Pinhas Peli,
        Pantheon Books. Copyright © 1991. With permission of
        Pantheon Books.

P. 97   *I Am Not...* From <u>A Living Covenant: The Innovative Spirit
        in Traditional Judaism</u> by David Hartman. Copyright © 1985
        by Free Press, a Division of Simon and Schuster. Reprinted
        with the permission of the publisher.

P. 97   *The Real Purpose*...From <u>The Sabbath</u>, by Samuel H.
        Dresner. Copyright © 1970. With permission of Burning
        Bush Press.

P. 98   *Shabbat — The Bride.* From <u>Bereshit Rabbah</u> 10.

P. 100 *I Need More Time.* By Ellen Goodman. Copyright © 1984, The
        Boston Globe Newspaper Co./Washington Post Writer's
        Group. Reprinted with permission.

P. 101 *A Time to Look..* from <u>Gates of Shabbat</u> by Mark Dov Shapiro.
        Copyright © 1991. CCAR Press. Used with permission.

P. 102 *All Wound Up.* By Jack Reimer

P. 103 *Renewal..* By Mordecai M. Kaplan, as adapted in <u>Likrat
        Shabbat</u>. Edited by Sidney Greenberg and Jonathan D. Levine
        © 1992 & 1973 by The Prayer Book Press of Media Judaica.

P. 104 *We Need Regeneration.* From "Judaism Looks at Life"
        by Hillel Silverman.

P. 104 *The Pause That Refreshes.* From <u>Heart of Wisdom</u> by Bernard
        S. Raskas. Copyright © 1979. With permission of Burning
        Bush Press.

P. 105 *The Sabbath Sets Us Free.* From "Kingdom Present" by
        Michael S. Kogan.

P. 105 *This is the Meaning*...From <u>The Essence of Judaism</u> by Leo
        Baeck. Schocken Books, Copyright © 1948.

P. 106   *Why We Nap on Shabbat.* From The Book of the Pious by
         Judah the Pious, 13c, #608.

P. 106   *No Task...*From The Forgotten Language by Erich Fromm.
         Copyright 1951, Copyright © 1979 by Erich Fromm. Reprinted
         by permission of Henry Holt and Co., Inc.

P. 107   *Sabbath the Queen.* By Hayyim Nahman Bialik, from Sabbath
         Day of Delight by Abraham Millgram. With permission of The
         Jewish Publication Society.

P. 108   *Free From the Chains.* From The Forgotten Language by Erich
         Fromm. Copyright 1951, © 1979 by Erich Fromm. Reprinted
         by permission of Henry Holt and Co., Inc.

P. 109   *Peaceful Hours.* From The Essence of Judaism by Leo Baeck,
         Schocken Books, © 1948.

P. 109   *Come Serenely to a Halt.* From Beyond Thyself by Hayim
         Donin. With permission of Charles Bloch Pub. Co.

P. 110   *Stop the World.* From How to Run a Traditional Jewish
         Household by Blu Greenberg. Simon and Schuster,
         Copyright © 1983 by Blu Greenberg. Reprinted by
         permission of Simon and Schuster, Inc.

P. 111   *How the Sabbath Differs.* From Turning East by Harvey Cox.
         Simon and Schuster Co, Inc. Copyright © 1977 by Harvey
         Cox. Reprinted by permission of Simon and Schuster, Inc.

P. 112   *On Shabbat...*By Neil Gillman for The Jewish Week,
         January, 1992.

P. 114   *The Day of Complete Harmony* From The Forgotten Language
         by Erich Fromm. Copyright 1951, © 1979 by Erich Fromm.
         Reprinted by permission of Henry Holt and Co., Inc.

P. 114   *The Biblical Equivalent.* From Turning East by Harvey Cox.
         Simon and Schuster Co, Inc. Copyright © 1977 by Harvey
         Cox. Reprinted by permission of Simon and Schuster, Inc.

P. 115   *We Need a Day of Rest.* From Faith by Louis Jacobs. Copyright
         ©1968. HarperCollins Publishers.

P. 115   *A "Fantastic" Idea.* By Sidney Greenberg.

P. 116   *A Family Experience.* From Knowing God: Jewish Journeys to
         The Unknowable by Elliot Dorff. Reprinted by permission of
         the publisher, Jason Aronson Inc., Copyright © 1992.

P. 117   *The Point to Rejoin Judaism.* From Knowing God: Jewish
         Journeys to The Unknowable by Elliot Dorff. Reprinted by
         permission of the publisher, Jason Aronson Inc., Copyright
         © 1992.

P. 117   *What was Created...*From Bereshit Rabbah 10.

P. 118   *How God Comforted...* From Sefer Ha-Agadah 381:22. by
         Hayim Nahman Bialik. Tel Aviv: Devir Pub.

P. 118   *The Useless Day.* Excerpts from <u>A Shabbat Manual</u> by W. Gunther Plaut are Copyright © 1972 by CCAR and used by permission.

P. 119   *A Precious Resource.* By Robert Gordis, "The Sabbath — A Precious Resource" <u>Judaism</u>, Vol. 31, #1 (Winter 1982). Reprinted by permission. Copyright 1982 by the American Jewish Congress.

P. 121   *Accept Our Gratitude.* By Ruth Brin as adapted in <u>Likrat Shabbat</u>. Edited by Sidney Greenberg and Jonathan D. Levine © 1992 & 1973 by The Prayer Book Press of Media Judaica.

P. 122   *To Love and To Care.* By Sidney Greenberg in <u>Likrat Shabbat</u>. Edited by Sidney Greenberg and Jonathan D. Levine © 1992 & 1973 by The Prayer Book Press of Media Judaica.

P. 123   *The Wondrous Rewards of Keeping Shabbat.* By Andre Ungar. Reprinted from <u>Siddur Sim Shalom</u>, edited with translations by Rabbi Jules Harlow. Published by The Rabbinical Assembly and The United Synagogue of Conservative Judaism. Copyright 1985 by The Rabbinical Assembly. Reprinted by permission.

P. 124   *The Gifts We Pray For.* Reprinted from <u>Siddur Sim Shalom</u>, edited with translations by The Rabbinical Assembly and The United Synagogue of Conservative Judaism. Copyright 1985 by The Rabbinical Assembly. Reprinted by permission.

P. 125   *Meditations Before Kiddush.* By Sidney Greenberg in <u>Likrat Shabbat</u>. Edited by Sidney Greenberg and Jonathan D. Levine © 1992 & 1973 by The Prayer Book Press of Media Judaica.

P. 126   *Meditations for Sabbath Candlelighting.* By Sidney Greenberg in <u>Likrat Shabbat</u>. Edited by Sidney Greenberg and Jonathan D. Levine © 1992 & 1973 by The Prayer Book Press of Media Judaica.

P. 127   *A Crowning Grace.* By Andre Ungar. Reprinted from <u>Siddur Sim Shalom</u>, edited with translations by Rabbi Jules Harlow. Published by The Rabbinical Assembly and The United Synagogue of Conservative Judaism. Copyright 1985 by The Rabbinical Assembly. Reprinted by permission.

P. 127   *Shabbat's Liberating Joy.* Reprinted from <u>Siddur Sim Shalom</u>, edited with translations by Rabbi Jules Harlow. Published by The Rabbinical Assembly and The United Synagogue of Conservative Judaism. Copyright 1985 by The Rabbinical Assembly. Reprinted by permission.

P. 128   *For My Family.* Composed by Navah Harlow. Reprinted from <u>Siddur Sim Shalom</u>, edited with translations by Rabbi Jules Harlow. Published by The Rabbinical Assembly and The

United Synagogue of Conservative Judaism. Copyright 1985 by The Rabbinical Assembly. Reprinted by permission.

P. 128   *The Profound Meaning of Being At One.* Adapted from the Zohar, Terumah. Reprinted from <u>Siddur Sim Shalom</u>, edited with translations by Rabbi Jules Harlow. Published by The Rabbinical Assembly and The United Synagogue of Conservative Judaism. Copyright 1985 by The Rabbinical Assembly. Reprinted by permission.

P. 129   *How Does Shabbat Bless Us?* Reprinted from <u>Siddur Sim Shalom</u>, edited with translations by Rabbi Jules Harlow. Published by The Rabbinical Assembly and The United Synagogue of Conservative Judaism. Copyright 1985 by The Rabbinical Assembly. Reprinted by permission.

P. 130   *How Does Shabbat Bless Us?* Based on words of Abraham Joshua Heschel. Reprinted from <u>Siddur Sim Shalom</u>, edited with translations by Rabbi Jules Harlow. Published by The Rabbinical Assembly and The United Synagogue of Conservative Judaism. Copyright 1985 by The Rabbinical Assembly. Reprinted by permission.

P. 131   *The Shabbat.* By E. Grindell, originally in <u>The Reconstructionist</u>, as adapted in <u>Likrat Shabbat</u>. Edited by Sidney Greenberg and Jonathan D. Levine © 1992 & 1973 by The Prayer Book Press of Media Judaica.